holding *grief*

A Dad's Memoir

DAN PENDER

Foreword by Owen Sheridan

Tangled Heart Press

THP and the THP colophon are registered trademarks of Tangled Heart Press

Produced by GMK Writing and Editing, Inc.
Managing Editor: Katie Benoit
Copyedited by Elizabeth Crooks
Proofread by Elexis Williams
Text design and composition by Libby Kingsbury
Cover design by Libby Kingsbury
Printed by IngramSpark

Print ISBN: 978-1-966981-24-4
Ebook EISN: 978-1-966981-25-1

Visit the author at www.danpender.com

This work was written, designed, and produced without the use of AI (artificial intelligence). Human creativity and intelligence may not be perfect, but they are far better than anything artificial.

Note: This publication is presented solely for informational, educational, and entertainment purposes. It is not intended to provide personal, relationship, legal, financial, or other advice and should not be relied upon as such. If expert assistance is required, the services of a professional should be sought. The publisher and the author and their affiliated entities and individuals do not make any guarantees or other promises as to any results that may be obtained from using the content of this book. To the maximum extent permitted by law, the publisher and the author and their affiliated entities and individuals disclaim any and all liability in the event any information contained in this book proves to be inaccurate, incomplete, unreliable, or results in any harm or loss. You, the reader, are responsible for your own choices, actions, and results.

Praise for *Holding Grief*

"I am a woman in recovery. Dan's story of love speaks to me in the space 'between.' His relationship with himself and his daughter, Julia Gene, nurtures my soul and develops my authentic self from the rubble in my sub-basement. He embraces fear hidden in a sacred space that cries out for me to be seen. His courage comes through despite how scary it is at times to listen and be silent. It empowers me to fuel my next steps, which are lived in the 'tangled unknown,' as he says.

[Dan's] generational 'systems story' is my story. I am the one that can [with my Higher Power] look at it, examine it, and move to embrace the beauty within. I am challenged to share this beauty with the hope it may help others, as Dan has done so intimately."

Anne, *a woman in recovery*

"Dan's sensitivity to his real relationship with Julia is deep, personal, and attentive. He is very much in the moment with her and himself. His writing challenges us with the fact that Julia is very much her own individual person who GIVES and RECEIVES with him as he with her. Julia attends to Dan, impressing upon him— teaching him how to touch, love, and be intimate. It's powerful!"

Owen Sheridan, *father and friend*

"Writing one's truth can be dangerous, healing, and freeing. I've experienced my partner of over twenty years tell his truth amidst love, pain, and forgiveness through his many years spent writing *Holding Grief.* This is a complex story of an unimaginable death of a child, a family system that demands their version of you, and a pain so deep most could not comprehend. Don't be surprised if you experience a cathartic cry that might just heal and set you free too."

Maggie Ernst, *partner and parent*

"I am so fortunate [at age ninety] to have read Dan's courageous story of love. Dan has my full support to talk about his story as part of our larger family story. My joy in reading this book is seeing him learn to use his sensitivity and tender loving touch to connect with so many."

Sheila Pender, *grandmother of Julia Gene and Dan's mom*

"As a lifelong friend and colleague, I've known Dan for fifty years. His contributions to human development and mental health are far too many to count. This book is not just the result of exemplary clinical skills and experience but the fruit of a life dedicated to the integration of self and the liberation of individual human potential, as evidenced in his own personal journey into the depths of challenge and opportunity in family life."

Steve W., *father and colleague*

The proper function of man
is to live,
not to exist.
I shall not waste my days
in trying to prolong them.
I shall use my time.

—JACK LONDON, *Credo*,
San Francisco Bulletin, 1916

To Mary Ellen,
devoted and loving mother,
and
our five wonderful children.

GRATITUDE

My gratitude goes out to the Phoenix House of New England staff who supported and encouraged me over the past two decades to generously serve those seeking and maintaining their recovery and mental health.

I appreciate my partner of over twenty years, Maggie Ernst, for her passionate support of me. She sees me for who I am and who I am becoming. I am grateful to her for seeing me and for her many editorial contributions to this book. She is present both within me and within these pages.

I am the person that I am today, and continue to become, due in large part to the therapeutic support of my former family therapist, Bruce Anspach. It was in encounters with him that he introduced me to the many family therapy concepts and interventions from which I have benefited. It is my hope that I have integrated what I have learned into these pages and that it will benefit you.

I am grateful for the ongoing love and support of my children and their partners that make life so worth living. I share gratitude with my children's mother, without whom this story of love could not have been lived and written. I give special recognition and appreciation to my siblings, their partners, and their children, who all continue to evolve with me in claiming the value of what it means to be family.

Finally, thank you, Mom and Dad, for the lives you have lived, showing us that redemption is possible to both claim and share through acts of kindness despite difficult paths forged.

CONTENTS

FOREWORD

by Owen Sheridan

Dan is my friend.

Dan and I first met in the fall of 1972, as naïve high school freshmen boys who uprooted ourselves from home, friends and family to study—ostensibly—for the Roman Catholic priesthood at a seminary in a small town in Pennsylvania. Like many of our classmates, we arrived there for a mix of reasons, most of which we were barely conscious of, ranging from trying to meet adult expectations, to escaping aspects of restrictive or oppressive home life, to seeking self and autonomy, and so much more.

I hailed from the same small farming town in which the seminary itself was situated. Dan came from Brooklyn, the borough of churches, the land of stoops, stickball, and sewer caps. To say we became fast friends would be misleading. I initially found Dan's Brooklyn brashness and street smarts intimidating; offensive, even. My own introversion and robotic desire to please and perform were tough to crack. And given how the seminary segregated its students, opportunities for genuine connection were few—often serendipitous, certainly hard won. Yet we did, we have, and we continue to do so.

While our paths have taken different courses through the years since, I have come to deeply respect and value Dan for his brute honesty, his savvy, his uniquely insightful and intuitive mind and heart—and for his care and friendship. Dan is one who explores where many of us retreat. He feels where many of us remain numb.

He articulates where many of us are confused or speechless. He follows hunches, questions, and challenges where many of us would rather withdraw and scroll our phone feed.

A fully human life, well lived, pulls you down—*katabasis*: the mythological descent into darkness and ashes through which alone we may rise toward wholeness. While I am a parent, I can only poorly imagine what the loss of a child feels like, especially one so young, so dear, so innocent as Julia Gene, Dan's daughter. I had the great honor of being invited by Dan to attend and share some music at the memorial service they held for Julia Gene. What I vividly recall is that feel of unspeakable sadness, the gaping chasm of grief that threatens to swallow all in its proximity. Crushing. At the same time, I remember all of the poignant signs of life: the simple, silent, loving touch and glances; the thoughtful, unwasted words, embraces, and shared silence; and young Kevin's disarmingly boyish presence and openness among all of these grown-ups. Graciousness. Life comes at us laden with loss—grief, sadness, death, trauma, violence, neglect, abuse. It brings us to our knees. What do we do then?

Much of what we are taught—by family, friend, and pastor, or by our ever-increasingly technological youth- and celebrity-obsessed culture—is to flee from this descent, to grossly simplify or sentimentalize it, or to so identify with it as to be forever mired and lost. Much of what we are offered in this way has all the depth, sophistication, and nuance of a Hallmark Christmas special or a pop celebrity recently discharged from "rehab"—leaving us deceived, disillusioned and alone. You won't find that here.

Yes, Dan is well degreed, grounded in years of formal education and mentorship. Yes, he brings decades of experience from his work in family systems theory, spirituality, and human development. Most poignantly, however, Dan's gift to us in these pages arises from the depth, authenticity, and authority of his own lived experience; accompanied by that same Brooklyn brashness and honesty, tempered by care, insight, and hard-earned gentleness and humility taught to him by his daughter Julia Gene, by his son Kevin, and by his own child within. As Isaiah prophesied: "a little child shall lead them." In the end, through all the heartache, loss, and joys, there are no words, simply gratitude.

This book is one man's journey; at the same time, it is yours and mine. Dan has a rare gift for articulating complex and nuanced human experience and system insight in language that is accessible and inviting. I read and experienced it as an invitation to step into my own memory—my own brokenness, grief, and pain—with like courage, openness, and humility. I encourage you to do likewise with a bit of advice.

Take your time. This is not a book to "finish," nor one to "get to the end of." It is an ongoing journey. Take it in small bites, as Dan offers them up to you here. Let them simmer. Savor them. Ruminate. Dream. Follow their lead. Take a companion with you, be it a journal with yourself, a trusted friend in conversation, or your god in prayer. Let it provoke you toward communion.

Finally, take off your shoes.

This is holy ground.

Owen Sheridan
December 2025

PREFACE

Holding grief speaks to a process of managing loss in your life. It is embracing, in however way you are able and ready, the variety of loss stages and opportunities for change. Loss invites grief to be held, experienced, nurtured, and challenged. One's perspective is altered, tangled, turned upside-down, inside-out, and all-around. This new viewpoint imposed by the loss alters how you view life in yourself and in others. For me, key relationships, especially with my partner and children, were altered. Our new point of connection or withdrawal (and all that is between) had to be revised, renegotiated. The loss shifted the family kaleidoscope, never to return to what it was before. A new paradigm existed, offering the past, present, and future to become as one—*now*. Holding grief invites this *new* now. It offers living-in-the-moment in a way twisted and all-tangled-up. Holding grief is all about slowing down to trust and love yourself in order to best love others. It's about real listening to what was, is now, and longs to be. Holding grief is a restorative, calming, supportive, and connecting presence through difficult times. With grief held by you and others, new possibilities emerge; a new perspective emerges to see and experience life as it continues.

How we hold our grief in this destabilizing movement is both a solitary and communal experience. We've been told to brace for impact after the initial drop in the water, as if the pain will dissipate shortly, but there are residual ripples in which the impact and loss linger. We are ill prepared to survive or thrive in the wake of its powerful challenge to emerge into someone or something else. What existed before the first ripple is no longer.

Questions emerge regarding our very identity. Can I remain as I was? Or is this ripple effect allowing or mandating me to become someone new? The test of time clearly depicts evolution in plain sight if one is willing to see. The sight of new possibility from the former is what my story of love offers. My story is part of your story. Our ripples interconnect and flow through one another, not unlike how families interconnect and influence one's very identity as it forms over time. Some in a family system may want to hold onto the old, expecting and even demanding neither of you to change, despite the experience of loss and holding grief.

Systems attempt to recalibrate us back to status quo. They count on no one changing unless it is prescribed by the family. This myth is shattered by the ripples. We are constantly challenged to adapt to their calm and intensity. One thing I know for sure is that the ripples of love and pain demand to be experienced. How we hold and support our grief ripples over time can impact other ripples. The encounter of overlapping ripples offers new possibility.

My story of love and pain is not original. The interlocking story lines created within our birth family, our family of choice, and our multigenerational family all combine to influence the mapping of what has been, is present, and can become. Your role is strongly influenced by these, but ultimately you define you. You are more than your family role. You possess a unique position and voice to effectively become who you are intended to be, flowing within the ripples and waves of life. How you hold grief and loss significantly impacts who you are and how you influence others. Ours is not a solitary journey. If we become open to the ripples of life-and-death surrounding us, we can emerge the better for it. We cannot effectively wish for what was. That now is our past. Present living faces that past, forging a new path into the future. We need to hold our grief, supported and nurtured to become something—perhaps someone—new.

My journey within these pages describes the pull of how my family system needed me to be when facing the most difficult circumstance of loss. What another person needs me to be often works to sustain their way of life. They do not have the last word when it comes to improving my best self. I shaped my story, which did not happen alone. The intimate relationship I have with myself and others helped weather the storm, its aftermath, and the rebuilding of life itself.

My story had many twists and turns that challenged me to name what happened; to see the truth in action and respond. Of course, my first instincts were to react, in many ways, reinforcing my system identity (that which others want and need me to be for their existence). Fortunately, I had relationships that helped me discover my narrative of who I am or, as I like to say, who I am intended to be. After all, how we play the hands we are dealt is what really matters.

Overview

In Part One, titled "Holding Grief—A Dad's Memoir," I share the story of the intimate relationship I had with my second child of five. In 2025, the year of her 34th birthday, I undertook my third major effort to gather—in some cases, rewrite—our continuing story of love.

I began writing the story over thirty years ago. The original first six chapters were written by me, a practicing marriage and family therapist. The remaining chapters were co-written with my wife,

Mary Ellen (nicknamed Mellon), a registered nurse who specialized in labor and delivery. We collaborated on this project together for the purpose of the column I wrote for our local newspaper, the *Agawam Advertiser News*, some ten years after we had lived the experience. The story of love, as I referred to it, was preceded by nearly a hundred columns in the same newspaper. Those columns are companion writings that set the stage for understanding my actions taken within the story of love. The story of love itself was first published in the "For Your Health" section of the *Agawam Advertiser News*, on January 18, 2001. Below is a link to the archived columns:

https://archive.org/search?query=%22dan+pender%22+%22Life+Through+Stories%22+&sin=TXT

The weekly column, which consisted of 500 words, ran for one and a half years under the banner *Let's Talk About It*. Later, it was changed to *Life Through Stories*.

Mellon, to whom I am no longer married, made invaluable contributions to the original newsprint columns. Our story of love could not be told without the part she played. Twenty-five years later, I invited her to participate in the creation of this book, but she declined. At first, I felt disappointed; then it became liberating as it opened up multiple opportunities. I revisited my original notes and began to rewrite and reformat portions of the original text, making our experience clearer. I was also able to include unwritten sentiments that I have felt since the works were published.

Mellon and I often agreed that our daughter provided many gifts to us. As we have moved forward, I believe our daughter remains present in her mother's decision to not participate in the creation of this book.

My philosophy is that book clubs have a life and breath all their own, which is why I created Part Two, "Book Club Discussion." In this section, I offer a framework for leading groups from a method learned in my study of Carl Rogers, an American psychologist and the founder of person-centered therapy. I have modified the name of his Reflective Listening method, referring to it as the "Reflective Listening Leadership Book Club Model." I believe this method may be applied nicely here for those seeking a more structured guide to inspire group leadership and full participation.

There are many variations of Rogers' model. A commonality they share is how essential it is to listen to what each person is saying. Once an individual has spoken, the group repeats what they heard to ensure that they were listening and understood the meaning. After all, don't people just want to be listened to and heard?

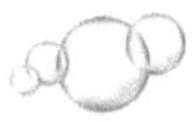

Over the years, I've sometimes had a difficult time letting go of roles that no longer fit my stage in life and circumstances, like those of peacekeeper and problem-solver, particularly being a middle child. These roles helped me stay safe but were not mine to hold any longer. I have learned how to trust what's real, not just what's expected. My strength and power are gained by no longer holding on. My rope of trust must first be held by me before I am able to entrust it to someone else.

I entrust my story of love to you. I hope it supports your journey of self-discovery, love, recovery, healing, and growth. Here's to becoming our best self.

—December 2025

Introduction

GETTING TO KNOW THE AUTHOR

To begin, I am sharing four brief vignettes of self-love from my newspaper columns that set the context for how the added pebbles tossed in the water of my recovery story shaped who I am.

You in Recovery?

A pebble dropped. The first ripple emerged from a surprise encounter with a young lady with whom I had only exchanged a passing greeting upon her arrival to the substance use recovery home where I was the program director for ten years. She attended a contemporary song lyric recovery group that I led. During a song she interrupted, demanding, "You in recovery?"

I replied, "I've never tasted coffee or tried cocaine! But, aren't we all in recovery for something?"

This young woman was not the first or the last person to ask me that question. Each question and subsequent response carry their truth in the ripples, seeking the final destination of a shoreline. Over the years I developed this standard response, which sparked some to impatient insistence for a direct answer, while others took it as an opportunity to consider my response more deeply. Either way, a connection in the waters of recovery propelled the ripples forward.

For many, the "You in recovery?" question went to the heart of how I could be leading a treatment group on recovery if I myself were not a self-proclaimed recovering addict. The larger assumption was that only someone who walks the walk can talk the talk.

My challenge to those who asked was, "Doesn't your experience guide your walk on this path? Cannot folks share and benefit from different stories of addiction and recovery? One story tells of drinking from brown, blue, or green beer bottles while another from only white liquor bottles. Another story leads down a path of taking pain pills, while still another speaks to shooting up heroin."

I continued, "Despite our differences, how do we share similarities of experience through supportive talk? Can we talk about the commonality of what pulls us into destructive behavior? Can we consider how to support one another to achieve healthier patterns of living? Can we share what works from the many recovery resources available to accomplish getting unstuck and become freer to be our best self?"

I served within the substance use and behavioral health field for over thirty years, and my staff and patients alike often questioned me directly or asked each other in hallway conversations, wondering the same thing: "Is Dan in recovery?" Sometimes I felt like Captain John Miller, the lead character played by Tom Hanks in the movie *Saving Private Ryan*, whose servicemen had a secret pool guessing what the captain's job had been before the war. In my case, it seemed possible that my staff or patients had a similar secret pool guessing whether or not I was in recovery.

The young woman who asked me the "You in recovery?" question in the contemporary song lyric recovery group asked the same question about the members of Mumford and Sons, the band whose song "The Cave," provided the lyrics under review that day. I then found myself surprised by a turn in events that had never occurred, nor has it since. I provided her with my standard response, but nothing standard followed. As I led the group through listening to the song's powerful and inspirational lyrics of pain, despair, and hope something different surfaced in me.

I could not help becoming overwhelmed with my own personal truth of recovery and feelings of recurrent pain, despair, and hope regarding my second child. My emotions swelled as I remembered the events surrounding my daughter's life.

Little did I know, but my nonverbal, emotional response to listening to the song was visible to a patient, who tenderly and intimately asked, "Mr. Pender, are you okay?" The group paused from their self-reflection and all eyes were on me. I attempted to use the best of my professional skills to help redirect the focus back onto what they were addressing, as this was their group and not a time for me to pull their attention.

Something unexpected happened. This same patient, who intuitively saw me, simply invited me to respond to the same lyrics I had just invited them to ponder and tell my story. Without waiting for my response, she proceeded to recite select lines from the lyrics.

I teared up as she spoke those words aloud. I intensely felt my pain and despair as if the event had happened yesterday. For I knew my journey of recovery had been long, dating back to May of 1991. I became acutely aware of the boundary line I was up against in this moment. I had always professionally held firm my boundaries regarding self-disclosure, yet I also needed to trust the benefit of this personal invitation. I trusted myself and the group process in this moment, allowing my humanity to be visible.

I opened up and responded to her invitation. I shared how the grief we hold has a ripple effect of love and pain. I spoke about the feeling those lyrics raised in me each time I reflected on them in previous groups I had led. This pain and despair changed my life as I screamed in rage standing beside my newborn daughter in her sterile hospital room as she barely held onto life. My anguish ricocheted through the adjacent rooms and hallways, but mostly my screams terrified me. The power, volume, and shaking that accompanied my screams were foreign to me. It was as if I were having an out-of-body experience looking in on this young tormented father. He screamed at God to take him instead of his daughter, bargained to trade places to save his second-born child, and desperately offered to give his own life to save another.

I told the group how I felt like Jesus, who pleaded with his Father to take his cross from him and ultimately gave his life to redeem others. My pleas seemed to go unanswered. Suddenly, I began to notice from the corner of my daughter's tiny mouth, covered with tape securing a breathing tube, emerging bubbles.

She was talking to me in her bubbles and I listened.

I struggled to understand her response at first, as no answer came to me. I shared with the group my experience of not knowing how to understand her bubbles and how eventually I came to know what my daughter was saying to me.

Through my recovery, I continue listening to what I refer to as "Julia's call" and my response. I learned how to "let go and let God," slow down and listen to my soul's pain, despair, anguish, and love. I began to hope. I did not run from hope; instead, I ran toward it. Hope revealed itself to me. By not running away from my feelings, as I had often done in the past, I remained courageously feeling my loss in the moment. Somewhere along the way I embraced hope. I described to the group how I experienced two seemingly opposite sides of a coin—loss and hope—at the same time. I revealed that this was the first time for me that both feelings not only co-existed but fostered growth. I told them that I called this living "both-and" as opposed to "either-or." Either-or living permits experiencing only one or the other feeling. This experience of living with both loss and hope with my daughter helped me become more than I had been before. I was better able to gently forgive myself, continue my recovery, and transform into a deeper trust to become my best self. I ended by sharing that this type of both-and living was the greatest gift my daughter had given and continues to give me and others.

The same young female patient who had challenged me earlier shared, "It was very inspirational and helpful to witness your recovery in action. Thank you for being honest and telling your recovery story." Others provided similar feedback. The focus transitioned back to the song and sharing what was on the patients' hearts and minds.

One of my key takeaways that day was to trust living in the moment. This allowed me to be surprised by a real connection with a stranger. I saw how telling my story could empower the discovery of something helpful, good, and new that gave hope both to others and to me.

Nothing to Say

I have sat in my chair for nearly two hours now, facing a blank screen. Nothing is coming this late at night. I have no inspiration to write. Nothing is pressing. No personal or professional life issue weighs on me that I want to write about or feel safe enough to share with my readers.

I spent the first hour rereading old stories from my journals and essays from old writing classes. The material is honest, good, and painfully alert to the finer details of real living, capturing what was emerging in my mid-life. I glance at my blank screen and note the time in the upper right corner—12:30:09 a.m.

I'm tired from a long weekend of guests mixed with work. My usual pattern of carved-out time to write this column was side-tracked in favor of long-distance relationships. So, I lean back in my chair, pinch my legs under the table's edge so as not to recline too far, and begin to close my eyes, just for a minute. I convince myself this will be good for me. Something will come if I just take a few minutes to rest my eyes.

The temperature is chilly as I suddenly become aware of my neck snapping back over the headrest, mouth dry and wide open, breath labored and no sensation in my crossed legs. I slowly open my eyes, re-establishing my surroundings, convincing myself that the blank screen was just a dream. I fear leaning forward, convinced I am going to fall, thinking my feet will not hold me up.

My back cracks as I inch my way forward. Suddenly, it feels like I have no hands. My mind is not yet alert. I convince myself that I can safely reach out to hold myself up as I touch the edge of the desk, when suddenly I realize my hands are snugly tucked just inside my pants' belt. The spring of the chair takes over and gravity flings me forward. Pins and needles attack my extremities. I recover to look up at my reality; a blank screen, clock ticking, 1:43:36, :37, :38, :39, and counting.

TIME IS SLIPPING AWAY.

What do I *do*?

My deadline is just a few short hours away. Do I just forget about writing something new this week? Reuse something old like a reworked Christmas story and hand it in? But who wants to hear a Christmas story days after New Year's anyway?

It's now 2:06:05 a.m. and counting. I'm more tired, but at least the screen is not blank anymore. This must be good. I will have something to hand in soon, even if it's not my best writing. It is good that at least my opening sentence is no longer just out of reach. It's easy to convince myself that I have nothing to say, certainly nothing that matters to anyone else.

I sit here writing, thinking that people will now figure out who I really am—no one special. Certainly not the MVP (most valuable player/person) I spoke about in last week's column. Could I dare go there? What would happen if I let people know the internal pressures that drove me to near-perfection in sports, no matter the cost? Could I let people really know how starved I was for attention from my father, who showed up at nearly every game drunk?

The internal tapes and messages once again begin to play:

If only…

I had tried harder.

Perfected this or that pitch despite how much it hurt and was slowly injuring my immature pitching arm.

Dismissed the physical pain I continually endured in my knees that I only later discovered had minimum cartilage.

Never appeared weak.

Never told anybody about the pain or showed anybody my fear.

Never cried about the deep feelings of loneliness and isolation that accompanied receipt of all my awards and trophies.

Always appeared as if I had it all together and

Always maintained my high athletic skill and achievements as a way of one-upping my older brother, no matter the cost to me.

This was the flip side to being the MVP and it had a cost. I struggle to overcome that cost and maintain the goodness and self-value I have worked so hard to achieve. I write this early-morning message to you (most of whom I don't know and will probably never know) about something so personal and terrifying to face, hoping that it may help someone out there. But I also write for me, without the paralyzing fear of what you think of me or might say if we ever met.

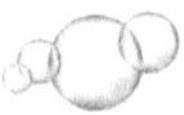

I recall during my preteen and teen days buying into the idea that I had nothing valuable to say and that I was a fraud. Many tender days and years later, I have grown into greater self-love. I now know being a fraud is my family's version of me, not mine.

Not even a blank page will stop me from knowing the truth of my own worth, even if I end up writing about

nothing to say....

It's now 2:32:12 a.m. and the baby is crying.

It's my turn as I realize that...

I DO have something to say.

I DO

As the time for marriage nears its date, time, and location, but before you get to say "I DO," many faith traditions conduct a public announcement of the upcoming nuptials. This communication provides a notice to anyone who might have "just cause" or reason why these two people should not be married. It requires coming forward to provide the pertinent information to assist determination as to whether or not the wedding will move forward. This well-known tradition is also done for candidates eligible to be ordained a Catholic priest. Various parish publications announce the details of the candidate's ordination several weeks in advance and invite response from the public.

It happened in my final year of seminary college, which was my ninth and final year in seminary formation. It was my second full year in the temporary vows that provided a trial period before taking the final vows of poverty, chastity and obedience. These vows are part of the religious order's preparation into priesthood, still a few years removed.

During this juncture, I was also considering whether I was going to continue forward in my vocation toward final vows and ordination to priesthood or leave the religious life. Over the years, the idea of leaving weighed on me. Because of yet another thing happening to me, I strongly leaned toward leaving this time, as it appeared it was the only way out to make it stop. But this time, it seemed different. Would I be leaving for me or yet again running away from it all?

Then came *The Announcement.*

I was holding on to "just cause" information about one of the ordination candidates. What should I do? Should I finally tell the administration or just keep trying to forget? Were others in the same boat as me or was I alone? Would I be alone if I responded to the announcement? That couldn't be possible, I convinced myself. There were too many of us.

I can't forget. I do remember!

I remembered what he repeatedly did to me. He was three years my senior and I looked up to him. Everyone did, especially the priests. He could do no wrong. Was he the model seminarian, as many thought, or just another perpetrator dressed in black and wearing a collar? My stomach was in knots. I couldn't sleep. I didn't know if I could have my voice, a platform, and visibility. I didn't know if someone out there wanted to listen to my story. Or was this announcement a mere formality without teeth?

I woke and made the call to the theologate graduate seminary school in Upstate New York where he lived and was scheduled to be ordained. My call was received by the Prefect of Students, Father JD. He listened. Before I knew it, he had discreetly arranged a car to drive me from Connecticut to New York to personally meet with him that day. There was an urgency in his response. He took me seriously.

I told him everything, not only about this candidate, but about what I experienced with students still in formation under his care prior to their ordination candidacy. I spoke about the boys who were no longer in the seminary system whom I personally knew and who informed me about their experiences of inappropriate touch with this candidate. I also talked about other inappropriate touch going on among peers and by some priests with students. I spoke about the practice of "shipping" students—almost exclusively those from Latin America. "Shipping" during our high school seminary days was when leadership discharged a person, typically for an instance or accusation of homosexuality. One moment your classmate was sleeping in his dormitory bed, the next his bed was stripped down, his locker and desk empty, all personal effects collected, cleared out, and he was gone. He had been "shipped" home without even a chance to say goodbye. It was as if he had never existed.

As I look back at it now, I remember we were told not to talk about it. I don't recall white students ever getting "shipped" for getting caught in the act. Whites seeing other whites "doing it" or knowing about it were cloaked in the safety of the code of white privilege. Most of the priests were white. Although Father JD was white, he was an exception. He wanted to know the truth.

I was in the early stages of finding my voice and learning to trust myself. I was gaining courage to speak up, speak out, and learning to trust again. I trusted Father JD. He cared about what happened to me. He really listened to me. He wanted my full story. I was not invisible to him.

The pain and injustice the seminary system had inflicted upon so many was riddled with silence as remedy and discharge as solution. Father JD assured me that he was in a position to follow up with all the details I had provided. He said, however, that it was going to take some time since I was the first, and so far the only one, to speak up asserting how the seminary formation system was failing to acknowledge its truth.

He was true to his word. The notification came to everyone at the same time declaring that one of this year's ordination candidates was withdrawn and no longer at the seminary. I decided to leave religious life and not continue on to the theologate graduate seminary; years later I heard the high school seminary I had attended was closed. A few years after that, the college seminary I had attended closed its doors as well. Thereafter, so too did the theologate graduate seminary. All three parts of the system were shut down.

This all happened during a time when public news disclosures were just beginning to creep out about the clergy sex abuse scandal in parishes across the country. I like to think these seminary closures were due to the internal functioning of both the seminary and larger church systems' foundations being shaken to their core. I suspect that there were additional revelations of student-on-student and priest-on-student sex scandals. I believe my disclosures brought to light the need to reform the seminary formation system itself. These investigations and public disclosures brought to light the significant problems within the training grounds across our country of young men being prepared to serve as priests.

The local seminary administrators were not unlike the senior hierarchy leading the larger parish systems in how they addressed the same problem of inappropriate touch. As I experienced it, leadership simply moved the problem out of sight and out of mind and acted as if it never happened. Or in the case of my seminary situation, my priest counselor, who was also the Student Prefect, provided me with the "antidote" to my repeated sexual abuse.

"While on vacation," he told me, "go and have multiple girlfriends."

This guidance was given despite being strictly prohibited according to the rules. No dating was permitted while at home or with girls from town while at the seminary as part of the preparation to take the vow of chastity. In fact, the counselor's specific instructions were to have two or three girlfriends at the same time. For years I did as I was instructed, right up until I took my temporary vows. Then my confusion escalated. I no longer had the use of the "antidote" remedy as the sexual abuse persisted.

I left the religious life soon after my talk with Father JD and receipt of my college diploma. I left fearful that I would be retaliated against. I was afraid my name would get out as a whistleblower. I thought I left for me, but like leaving home when I was twelve, I once again reached for a parachute, whisking me away from a bad situation attempting to protect myself.

I have regretted leaving the seminary for over forty-four years and have been carrying this unwritten column since. My call to priesthood and religious life did not disappear when I left that May graduation day in 1981. I could not, however, continue in a system where I was invisible and reconciliation seemed impossible because it never happened. But it did happen. Not even my desire to answer the call could rewrite history. So, I freed myself to travel a new path and my confusion persisted. Which way do I go? What do I do with my life? What is my new function? How do I navigate such confused sexual identity? How do I avoid repetition of the abuse? What skilled job can I do straight out of the seminary? To whom do I say, "I DO?"

I said, "I DO" three years after leaving the seminary. I was married for eighteen years and then divorced. I was blessed with five amazing children. I then said "I DO" to a loving partnership—although not a marriage—with a gifted, wonderful woman with three terrific children of her own, which has evolved these past twenty-plus years now.

The single most important "I DO" is the one I affirm to myself.

I DO trust myself.
I DO trust others to hold the other end of my rope
because I first trust myself.
I DO have the courage to speak my voice.
I DO see myself and am okay being visible in your sight.
I DO have the courage to own my TRUTH as best as I
can recall, express, and claim it.

As my former therapist Bruce Anspach reminded me during a recent reconnection after informing him of my pending publication, he stated, "The family doesn't want you to tell the truth!"

I know telling the truth about others and myself is a risky and dangerous proposition, but it can be even more so if I do not tell my truth. Choice, freedom from chains, claiming and caring for my true scent-of-self (I'll explain that term in the next section) are worth my pursuit.

My Let's Talk About It columns, which include my story of love, are about facing my self in as honest and truthful a manner as I am able. I have learned that my uncertainty provides me with at least one point of clarity; confusion and ambivalence are guide-posts along the paths where past, present, and future converge in now moments. I claim each moment as precious, knowing that intimate moments in life-and-death are two sides of the same coin. I embrace these mutual gifts. I proclaim my life-altering discovery, I DO have something to say.

The Scent of Self

Can I smell myself? Well, let's see.

The term "scent-of-self" captures the essence of who I am intended to be, as opposed to the "familial scent" that obligates me to live out the role and function I was born to serve. There is an intrinsic difference between these two scents. Each is like an identified smell that both receives and disseminates how we relate within systems. The familial identity serves primarily the survival between the generations, while living your scent-of-self has generational consequence. I have described the latter in terms of an ever-changing kaleidoscopic family process. Move the kaleidoscope one turn and the whole picture changes.

Is it even possible to be an individual?

If individualism is achieved, can I sustain and live it within relationships? What happens if I become more than my family role and function?

I will describe in my forthcoming book how this new feeling or scent-of-self is as if you no longer exist, exiled into the desert experience no longer able to return back to the familiar.

Who are we without our familial ties?

This journey will include risk. The pressure remains to re-create one's family role in relationships with friends, strangers, co-workers, church members, and social organizations. Becoming the scent-of-self, the person you are intended to be is radical, especially amidst the family's pressure to have you remain in service to their needs.

I will talk about the importance of achieving your scent-of-self by being connected to, yet separate from, your family. The familial scent would have you abandon any notion that change or becoming your best self is possible.

You need to decide if change is possible.

Is becoming an individual an imperative in your life? Are you willing to live beyond the family's expectation of you? Can a family be a family of unique individuals or is the collective identity more essential? Is there such a thing as choice or freedom?

The ties that bind!

Do you still have confidence in the face of doubt? Do you still have clarity in the face of ambivalence? Do you still have knowledge as you face the land of the unknown? If so, continue the work to discover your scent-of-self that claims true intimacy and share it, even with your family. This journey is possible and invites a new way of closeness with self and family that is not "fused" or "cut off." The scent-of-self is more easily self-identified over time, open to visibility and feedback from others. Pursuing this scent requires incremental change. It is not a one-off. It invites a greater vulnerability into the depth of trust mixed with caution. It becomes a way of life that includes knowing the difference between these two scents.

The familial scent, on one hand, requires living out your family role and identity, often to the detriment of your true self. Expect the family system to try directly or indirectly to pull you back from yourself, whether in close proximity or geographic distance. If they are not successful in pulling you back, don't be surprised if you collude with them or nonfamily relationships to move away from yourself to get that "back-at-home" feeling. The familial scent experience is clear: Be who we need you to be and put us first, ahead of yourself.

The scent-of-self, on the other hand, acknowledges the needs of the family, but places self-care as the priority. It is all about responding to self and not reacting to the lure of the system's needs.

The smell test is important.

Which scent are you responding or reacting to? Knowing and naming which is which is essential. Following the scent-of-self creates both—and living where you both make your own choices and live your own life. It is free to be both connected to and separate from the binds that stick. Each day is an opportunity to know more than your family identity/role and become more of your best self. You need to know this difference!

The scent-of-self beckons intimate in-the-moment living.

When visible, don't be surprised if you are asked, "Are you telling me that you smell yourself?" Exactly! Be your smell. Acknowledge the unacknowledged. Accept and pass on your scent. Claim freedom from the chains that bind. Become and live the way you choose. Own your own achievements and mistakes as you become who you want and are created to be. Take courage to name and reveal your scent-of-self. Sustain it by trusting yourself to see your real self. And finally, share it with others. This is the essence of the "problem with goodness" that is a worthy problem to embrace.

I conclude introducing myself via providing background context to our story, Holding Grief, by offering you another newsprint column from my Let's Talk About It series entitled…

The Problem with Goodness

What is he talking about now? A problem with goodness? Actually, I believe there are a few problems with goodness that are worth our consideration. Allow me to set the context. Last week, a reader gave some feedback to one of my earlier columns and raised these questions: How good can I have it? and Can I have it all? The simple answer is: sure, you can have it all and have it as good as you'd like. The more complex answer involves, I think, going deeper into the nature of goodness in oneself and as it pertains to relationships.

One place to start when considering goodness is what it is related to, namely, badness. In place of badness, we might use words like evil, sadness, unhappiness, feeling down, or being unaware. Being aware of how bad things are can be a way of not facing the potential of goodness. Often these negative feelings or behaviors, like bad habits, leave us with little room for personal choice. We might be faced with a problem of hitting or yelling at our children or partner and would like not to do this but feel stuck and unable to make the necessary changes we desire. These negative feelings and behaviors are often powerful influences in our life and in how they impact those important to us. The same can be said about the power of goodness in our life and how it influences our relationships.

One problem I experience with the power of goodness in my life is coming to name what is good. At first, this might seem silly. Of course, we should be able to name what is good in our life. But if you are like me, often your negative or bad feelings and behaviors can sufficiently distract you from what you might otherwise want and see, namely, goodness.

Another problem that I experience with goodness in my life, once I have named it, is sustaining it. Keeping what is truly good for me and how good that is for those connected to me can be very challenging. Maybe I can have real happiness and contentment for a few minutes, hours, or even days, but so much seems to be working against me to move away from goodness and get back to something old that is not necessarily good for me.

This brings me to my third and final element of the problem with goodness, namely, having goodness in my relationship systems. What I mean, in more clinical terms, is the power of the family emotional system and its influence on my living and owning goodness in my life on my terms. Key to understanding how family emotional systems work is that they are not inherently bad, but for many of us, we experience our families as forces that attempt to strongly influence how we are to live our lives more on their terms than on our own.

I assume that a healthy scent-of-self is moving away from the family's view of how you should live and moving more into having your view of who you are on your terms. This does not mean that our families cannot be good influences to help obtain a healthy scent-of-self. Some people are fortunate in this way. Many others are not.

I will talk more on this problem of goodness in the coming weeks.

Your examples and feedback would be very helpful for our reflection on goodness as we try to concretely struggle with the problem of naming, sustaining,
being influenced by relationships and
the process of owning our unique goodness that is in each of us.

PART ONE

Holding Grief—A Dad's Memoir

Chapter 1

THE ARRIVAL

I have been traveling on a new road toward commitment and intimacy with my self since the birth of my second child. My journey has had many detours. I wouldn't have it any other way, except that I wish this stop could have turned out differently.

My second child was born three years ago as of this writing, on May 21, 1991. When I allow myself to remember the details, I recall how excited Mellon and I were at beginning the labor process, which went on through much of the night, and attending our regularly scheduled OB appointment the next morning. The fruits of labor were confirmed by the doctor and she instructed us to go directly upstairs to the labor and delivery room. We were moving right along, joyfully appreciating how the pregnancy had gone full term and how well the labor was going.

Later that afternoon, with Mellon's cervix dilated at eight centimeters, the fetal monitor detailed that dreaded deceleration in the baby's heart rate, similar to our experience with our firstborn, Kevin, who was born nearly two and a half months prematurely. We feared that what we experienced before was reoccurring. "Please, God, not again!" I could hear Mellon murmur almost under her breath. The word went out among the medical team—prep the operating room for an emergency C-section. Our hope for a VBAC delivery (vaginal birth after a previous C-section) was shattered. Mellon trembled with fear, exclaiming, "Not another section. No God, please no, please!"

Her pink and red face suddenly turned white. She knew what was really going on in the brisk, hushed whispers of the staff. Mellon was on the hospital staff as a labor and delivery nurse. These were her peers, her friends, who were frantically hurrying to prep her. After all, she was one of their own. She was their Mellon too.

The word spread like wildfire throughout the hospital. They all had anticipated with us the birth of "Penelope" Pender—the staff's pet nickname for the baby, since we had not yet chosen a name. (We affectionately referred to our baby as "HeShe.")

Grabbing for some ice chips, I struggled to swallow them. The surgical nurse abruptly moved me along into the operating scrub room to prep and gown. Dr. Kennedy and others stood quietly beside me, concentrating on how they would soon be helping my beloved Mellon and baby. I took my place in the operating room beside Mellon's head, which was partitioned off by a mini-curtain placed just above her chest. The curtain divided my care of Mellon and the other side, foretelling our birth story. Mellon had received a spinal anesthetic causing restricted mobility, but was fully alert. We were busy touching and crying, looking at one another, and praying that HeShe would be all right. Mellon was anxiously hopeful.

I tried to give Mellon some sense of the action on the other side of the curtain as she went in and out of her focused experience. I strained to stay in the moment, to stay out of the dreaded all-too-familiar family role of being the one in the middle. How could I simultaneously care for Mellon while trying to stretch over the curtain to give a piercing look beyond the sliced layers of tissue to our little one? I was so confused, yet so clear about my role in the moment: take care of them. This was not the time and place to feel scared or even consider myself.

I wondered, was this what it was like growing up, always caring more about "them," never learning to check in with myself to see how I was doing? Had nothing changed? Or was I navigating some new terrain by naming what was going on for me here and now, despite what was happening on both sides of the curtain? I had figured out that I could also care for the one in the middle. I was living out the ultimate win-win-win best-case scenario: caring for Mellon, our baby and me. A trifecta of love.

Looking into my wife's baby blue eyes, I said out loud in a whisper, violating the system that would have the emotion go unnamed, "Mellon, I'm so scared." Sweat poured down my face as I realized I was both present and in the middle, yet in a different sort of way. I was experiencing being part of a three-legged stool. I was one leg providing healthy stability to both sides of the curtain. Mellon was another, providing all she could do to bring forth life. The medical team was the third leg. Arriving soon to provide even more stability as a fourth leg was our son, Kevin. He was nearly five years old, nervously waiting with our friends at home for word of the birth, so he too could join this wonderful moment.

Finally, the surgical knife revealed life's truth. Our little girl was in stress, fighting for her brand-new life. The APGAR assessment measures five key components at birth: color, heart rate, reflexes, muscle tone, and respiration, each of which is given a score of 0, 1, or 2. Our little girl scored a 3 out of a possible 10 in that first minute of life. After the medical team swiftly applied suction to her mouth and massaged her blue body, she showed some sign of improvement. She was breathing, barely. Mellon and I were in clear view of our baby girl's struggle unfolding. It was a horrifying truth, one that I had no choice but to bear witness to, despite my best preparation for this moment. There was so much happening around me that I knew nothing about. Mellon knew. This was her zone. I didn't know what the ranges of the APGAR score meant, but Mellon's eyes couldn't lie. Her face told the story of her concern. I was shaking. We held each other's cold hands as we trembled with fear together. Nearly eight minutes passed after the preliminary APGAR measurement. Smiles tentatively began to emerge in the operating room as we awaited the magical familiar, rhythmic, and high-pitched cries that would signal healthy life was among us. Our little girl let out her first loud cry.

Our still unnamed precious bundle achieved an 8 out of 10 on her APGAR this time. She was brought over to us and we briefly snuggled, as Mellon was still limited in her movement due to the spinal injection.

Our fears turned to tears of joy and relief.

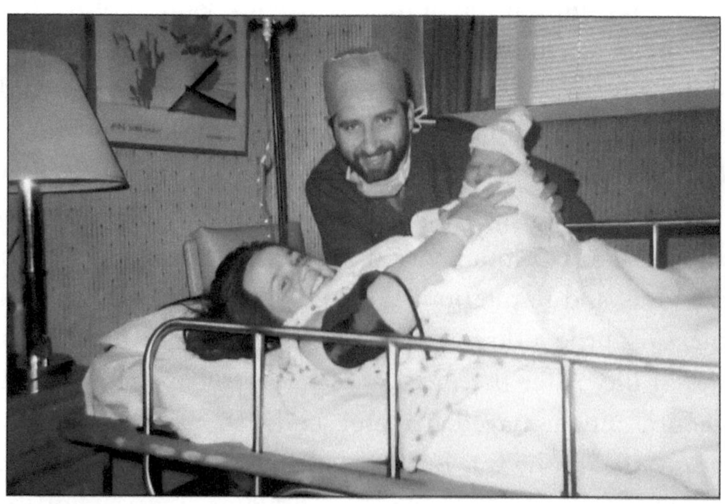

Chapter 2

I KNOW YOU

Suzanne, Mellon's labor and delivery co-worker and friend, was fortunately able to be with us during the delivery. Her day shift was coming to an end, as was our C-section. Her wonderful smile was reassuring during this time of uncertainty. Before leaving shift, she offered to go to our home and bring Kevin back to us to meet his sister. We accepted.

For the next sèveral minutes, the focus remained on completing the C-section and making sure Mellon was well taken care of. I had the chance to linger my attention on our baby girl. I stroked her soft, pink, and somewhat yellow skin as she soaked in the warmth of the lights above. I marveled at the miracle of Mellon's body transforming right before my eyes. Soon she was resting more comfortably. I too became more at ease as I moved more freely between the two sides of the curtain.

Before long, we were across the hall in Mellon's favorite room, number four. It was the largest of all the home-style delivery rooms and the furthest away from the hustle and bustle of the front desk. We enjoyed the quiet and privacy it offered.

I held my little girl for the first time. I loved it! I soon asked

Mellon if it were too soon to breastfeed, since the spinal anesthetic had not run its course and limited her motion but was told we could.

The attempts were cumbersome, yet no less marvelous. The miracle of life, baby seeking bonding and mama giving her nutrition. After several minutes of the baby's unsuccessful attempts to latch onto Mellon's nipple, they both grew discouraged, and I knew each needed a break before giving it another try.

The baby's frustrated cries continued as we removed her tightly wrapped pink blanket to briefly assure ourselves of her ten perfectly formed toes and fingers, all five pounds, twelve ounces, and nineteen inches of her. Her scattered strands of light reddish-blonde hair nestled under her hospital beanie cap. She was blessed with her mother's beautiful sky-blue eyes, now inquisitively gazing up as if to say:

I know you.

Kevin arrived just in time. He and his Little Sis immediately captured each other's gaze as she responded to his high-pitched tone that now resonated outside the womb for the first time. She responded with the high-pitched cry that we had just recently celebrated. Their first conversation was interrupted so the attending nurse could securely bundle her for the next one and a half hours. She stopped crying and I don't think Kevin ever stopped smiling. He jumped up into my lap on the recliner arm and assumed the position we had long rehearsed using Brownie, his stuffed bear. Both Mom and Dad were so proud of big brother Kevin. He cooed with anticipation as the nurse passed the baby to me and I placed her in his lap. Brownie sat beside him with his friend, Pinky-the-Bear.

Kevin wiggled his dangling feet as he engulfed this precious pink bundle of love that would forever change his life. Kevin had requested from Santa a pink bear for his new brother or sister, and Pinky arrived Christmas morning looking forward to this spring afternoon. Now Brownie and Pinky bubbled with pride as they appeared to smile up at their partners.

The family was all here.

Mellon remained flat on her back, the kids in the recliner, and me in the middle of yet another precious moment. We all took turns holding one another and enjoying the warmth and closeness of the new family blossom. Kevin didn't want to leave Sis. However, the babysitter and her parents soon arrived as our first visitors, just in time to photograph the magic of the moment. They would soon bring Kevin home to have dinner and ready him for bed, awaiting my arrival home for the night.

Before saying goodnight he asked us, "What is her name? Are we going to name her Michelle (his number one pick) or Molly (the name Mellon and I wanted)?"

I said, "I guess we haven't decided yet. Everything has been happening so quickly. Maybe we can decide together tomorrow morning when we come back to see Momma."

Kevin gently took off her beanie cap and ever so gently kissed his baby Sis on her forehead, saying in his sing-songy way, "I luvvv youuu baby sister. Goodnight. I'll see you tomorrow morning."

Chapter 3

THE GLASS WALL

Shortly after we said goodnight to Kevin, our nurse, Liz, took our baby down the hall to the nursery for the night. I recall going down to the cafeteria before it closed for a quick bite to eat. When I arrived back upstairs, Mellon's new room across from the nursery was ready. I packed up our things and escorted her (since she was still unable to raise herself from her bed) down the long corridor. With chart in tow, Liz pushed us toward the proud moment of looking through the glass wall that made up the expansive nursery window to catch a glimpse of our newborn daughter.

When we arrived at the glass wall; something was different about this picture. I knew this because I often dropped by the glass wall with Kevin when visiting Mellon at work during her pregnancy. We would always take the long walk down the endless corridor to peer through the glass wall to enjoy the newborns and giggle at how different they were from one another. I'd imagine with him that each newborn on the other side of the glass wall was ours. I remember lifting Kevin up on my knee. We'd gaze in to see how the babies were perfectly wrapped in their warm blanket envelopes. Some would even appear to be looking back at us. Soon, it would be our turn.

As we rolled past the glass wall, a scene that was in stark contrast to my previous visits with Kevin, I described to Mellon how

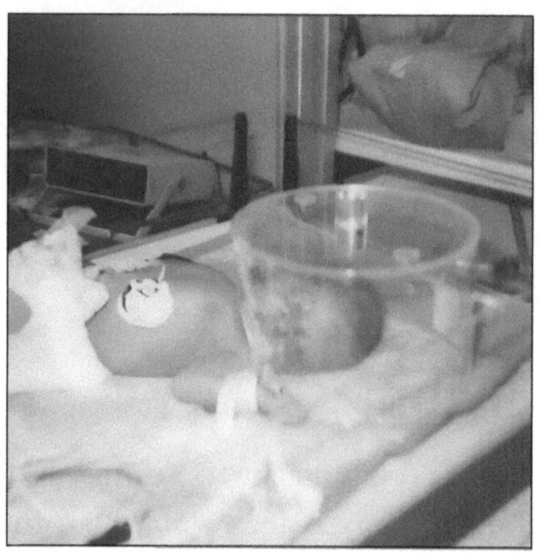

"baby Pender" was off in the back left corner with only a diaper on, exposing her to the overhead warming lights. I suspected this was cause for concern, as four or five medical staff huddled around her bedside. They were speaking quickly as their hands tore open this package and inserted that object; my worry intensified. Once again, I became confused, as I didn't know what was going on around me.

On one side of the glass wall was my wife, unable to lift her head and relying on me to tell her what was happening, and on the other side was movement like a silent movie without subtitles, leaving me to make out the dialogue and plot. This put me in the director's chair of a movie without a script. All I could do was attempt to interpret the various actions, instruments, and emotions. It was as if I was right back in my family doing the all-too-familiar and explicit job to "figure it out," communicate the uncommunicated and not get it wrong. I did my best.

We continued into Mellon's new private recovery room across from the nursery. The staff and I gently transferred Mellon from one bed to the other as comfortably as we could. As our room emptied, Liz went into the nursery to check on our baby. It was only minutes later before she returned, but it seemed like hours.

Liz said with a straightforward tone, "She's having trouble with respiratory."

Mellon replied, saying something to the effect of, "No problem—she did have some trouble with meconium. Maybe she has a touch of pneumonia—I can handle that."

As the pediatrician arrived, word came to us that the baby might have to be transferred to the local medical center. We didn't know what to make of this news. A couple of minutes later, the doctor informed us that he was hearing irregularities in her tiny heart. This disturbing news came only thirty short minutes after our great experience of bonding together with Mellon and Kevin. The pediatrician told us that he was calling for the medical center's transport team to come and further assess the baby's condition, but he was pretty sure that they would be moving her tonight.

He went on to say, "We'll be putting her on pure oxygen to assist her breathing for now. I'll keep you updated as more information becomes available."

What was worse, being forced into a C-section or this?

"Please God," we prayed, "be with our little one."

The worst was yet to come. Our baby was in trouble again.

I thought to myself, "Can we handle what will be next?"

Will the legs of our relationship stool hold as before?

Our tears began to flow.

Our hands once again became cold.

Chapter 4

THE ROAD AWAY

The transfer team dispatched with great urgency from Baystate, the local medical center. I was informed when they arrived. I went out to the glass wall to view their interaction with our baby, wondering what news we could expect.

They decided to transfer our little girl immediately. To our surprise, the transfer was not to Baystate, but rather south some thirty miles to Connecticut's Hartford Hospital, which has a pediatric cardiology department. Our baby's problem was her heart function.

Joanne, the nursery nurse, was the first to recognize that our little girl was in trouble when she began to turn blue. She assessed that there was certainly a respiratory problem and maybe more. The team continued to apply pure oxygen to temporarily relieve the pressure. They further assessed that the opening in her heart, the *ductus foramen ovale*, which naturally closes three or so hours after birth, needed to remain open. Medication temporarily kept it open to stabilize her circulation.

We had only minutes to digest the news, give our consent to treat, and say goodbye. Mellon said, "Before she leaves, we need to give her a name." The pressure to name her grew larger than we could ever have imagined. Somehow, the process and significance of naming our baby moved beyond just giving her a cute snappy name that we were pondering all along, like Molly. Certainly, any attachment to the staff's pet name "Penelope" was not good enough anymore.

What was her name to be?

Even though we had told Kevin we would see him in the morning and name her then, we knew what we had to do. We knew this was not Kevin's decision, but we were concerned for him. The name that almost immediately emerged from our discussion was Julia. This was a name on our short list and was clearly not a favorite of Kevin's. Mellon and I simultaneously nodded with agreement, joined by the knowledge of our unspoken common connection to the name Julia. It was popular due to the famed actress Julia Roberts, but both Mellon and I embraced the name Julia because our precious little one would carry the strength of my maternal grandmother's name, Julia Donahue, my Nannie.

Among her twenty or so grandchildren, there exists a second Julia Donahue, but our Julia was Julia Pender. Julia was Nannie's third great-grandchild and first to be named after her on the Pender side of the family. This was an honored position.

Then the most unlikely combination of names emerged. "Let's give her a middle name," I said. "How about Gene, spelled with a G, after my father, Eugene?" And, so, she was Julia Gene Pender.

Our tears confirmed this was the right choice.

Her name actually bridged the long-standing chasm between my mom's side of the family and my dad's side. I don't think we realized this or its significance to the extended families at the time, but our Julia Gene did in fact connect both families in a new way. We had bridged something not meant to be mixed, blending the strength of the matriarch—Julia—with the person many would say was the "problem," the "drunk," the "useless one"—Eugene.

Tension had always existed between these two individuals and between these two families. Now there appeared a little girl—Julia Gene—in the middle, like me. Maybe her role in life would be different from mine?

Julia Gene was wheeled into our room on a special transport bed that supported her inside an enclosed ecosystem. It completely covered her body, not unlike Snow White's plastic casket. Julia's head was inside yet another interior, cake-like helmet to provide the best possible environment for the pure oxygen flow.

Mellon was just able to slightly turn her body, as she was still recovering from the spinal anesthetic. I stood on one side of the container closest to the door, as Mom attempted to snuggle with her precious baby laying right next to her bed. The container allowed for two mini-openings to poke your arms through. Mellon was only able to bend over just enough to insert one arm into the container to stroke Julia's arms and legs.

I bent over to be at eye level with Mellon from the other side of the container. My peer captured the image of Julia's turned head facing Mom's. I mentally snapped a picture of this profound connection and separation. I watched Mellon stroke Julia's body as her own swollen, beet-red eyes flickered side to side as the team cautioned us to move along. Gasping for breath myself, I mourned this sight of mother and child still not bonded, still not held to one another, Mellon unable to penetrate the interior plastic helmet to give a farewell kiss to our baby's head.

It was all we could do to survive this gut-wrenching trauma

of our baby traveling the road away from us, not knowing if she'd survive the ride or the night. I don't remember how long we stayed together that night, shaking and sobbing.

Some friends of Mellon stopped in to extend their support. But the mood was as if Julia had died or we had died. Yet, the reality slowly set in that life was indeed holding on and hope remained. Mellon, exhausted from the ordeal, was finally able to fall asleep knowing that I would be remaining with her until receiving word from Hartford Hospital about Julia's safe arrival and set-up.

And so began the network of communication between us: Kevin being cared for by friends at home, Mellon remaining in recuperation from her C-section for at least three to five days in the hospital, and I traveling back and forth down to Hartford Hospital to connect Julia Gene to us and our extended family. The road away appeared lonely and uncertain and I was not sure I was strong enough for the ride ahead.

Julia, give me strength to travel this journey with you!

Chapter 5

THE CALL OF JULIA

"Julia," I sobbed, gasping for air.

"Julia," I shook uncontrollably.

"Julia," I finally managed to say in a slow, calm, reassuring whisper. I regained my breathing, gently stroking my tears from my cheeks.

I experience this sequence today, like a recurring dream, forcing me to remember that night after Julia's transfer. At times, I lie in bed at night still sobbing uncontrollably, attempting to face not only my memory of Julia, but my memory of me.

These last few months, years, I have been unwilling or unable to revisit the "call" of Julia. Perhaps this has something to do with my own struggle to continue writing our story. One night recently, I found myself flicking through television channels into the wee hours. Alone in the television glow, motionless toward caring for myself enough to go to bed, I remembered seeing on the program guide that *Brian's Song*, a TV movie about the life of football player Brian Piccolo and his death from cancer at age twenty-six, was on channel twenty-eight. I wondered if it was still on. So, I channel surfed and came upon its ending. That same ending I cried for when I first saw the movie many years ago. George Halas, the head coach of the Chicago Bears, spoke to the audience. His words remained with me this night as they did then, inviting the call of Julia once again. He said of the recently departed player Brian Piccolo, "Remember him not only in his death, but in his life." And so, I sobbed for my Julia, and I sobbed for me.

Julia—
you challenge me to face
your life-and-death
and
my Self
in our story of twelve days together
through 'til today.

Chapter 6

TENDER TOUCH

The morning after Julia's birth, I arranged child care for Kevin, visited Mellon in her hospital room, and was off to Hartford Hospital. Before going upstairs to visit Julia in her new surroundings, I first met with one of the staff's pediatric cardiologists. He said that Julia's transfer had gone well. She was resting comfortably and receiving medication to temporarily permit the ductus foramen ovale to remain open. He explained that we experience this process at birth when our fetal circulation seals itself off in order to get us ready to begin breathing on our own. Julia's hole had already closed but her heart wasn't working properly, which was why they needed to temporarily reopen the hole with medication. The doctor stated that surgery would be necessary to address the more serious problem they had diagnosed, Ebstein malformation, which is the rarest form of heart anomaly. One of Julia's ventricles was not properly formed and inhibited a proper flow of oxygen and blood. While the medication temporarily reopened the ductus foramen ovale, it rerouted the circulation to allow the other chambers of her heart to function normally. Her heart, however, could not sustain itself for much longer without what the doctor called a shunt bypass procedure. This would in effect, through the implantation of a specially designed tube, bypass the damaged ventricle and allow the heart to have the ductus foramen ovale sealed shut and function with only three chambers. The success rate for this procedure was very encouraging for newborns, the doctor said, and typically when the child reached the age of two or so, they would again perform surgery to modify the size of the shunt to account for normal physical development. Additional procedures would be performed as she naturally developed through the course of her life.

After my intense crash course in heart anatomy, including color overlays and other visual aids, the doctor informed me that their specialist who performed this highly sensitive procedure was out of the country and was expected back in a few days. Most likely, Julia's medication would continue to maintain her stable condition while they waited for the doctor's return. He assured me that they were proceeding to seek alternative openings in other regional hospitals capable of performing this procedure. Boston Children's Hospital, unfortunately, had no current openings.

So, by midafternoon, I finished up on the third floor and readied myself for the trip upstairs to my daughter on the fifth floor. I first called to check in on Kevin, then Mellon to briefly relay the information I had been able to absorb, and finally called family in Brooklyn to pass along current info before finding the elevator.

I couldn't understand why I was so scared. Here I was receiving relatively good news about my daughter's future, yet still I remained uncertain. The moments together with Julia that afternoon and the following morning amounted to five or so hours.

These moments in time are some of the most precious in my memory.

I knew I was doing something so unusual, so unfamiliar, so un-family-like for me. I was in the moment. It was just Julia and me, bonding, one-on-one. This opportunity was so unlike my opportunity to bond with my first child, Kevin. He was our two-and-a-half-month preemie. After his traumatic emergency C-section, he spent his first month of life residing in the neonatal intensive care unit. His allowance to come home "early" had everything to do with Mellon's tireless vigilance caring for him as if she were the lead staff member. Her rapport with staff guided a tremendous growth and resurgence by Kevin to rebound and even excel beyond all expectations. He was truly one of their success stories and Mellon had much to be proud of in her tender care and presence.

I could only marvel at how their bond propelled Kevin's healing and growth, so much so that the staff authorized discharge while Kevin was still under the minimal weight limit, all due to the effectiveness of Mellon's delivery of care. Unfortunately, his stay in the hospital and arrival home saw me working sixty hours or more a week at my Wall Street job and managing our three-story brownstone renovation project. I claimed small bites of time with him as I could. I was constantly playing catch-up, but Mellon pulled me into as many feedings as I could do. She expressed her breast milk and showed me how to bottle it at the appropriate volume and temperature. She was great at including me while I juggled everything else. I was giving as much as I could, but I missed out on so much with Kevin in those very early years. I was not going to let this happen again now.

At this point in time, I had the good fortune of having been very successful on Wall Street, so much so I was able to retire from that lifestyle in my mid-thirties. I moved my family out of the brownstone I had renovated to a newly built home in a small town in Massachusetts. So, when Julia's diagnosis came, I was fortunate and smart enough this time to choose her. I was in the middle of my graduate studies to become a marriage and family therapist. I suspended all my classes so I would not miss the opportunity to be in the most intimate of moments with myself and with this warm, now pink-skinned bundle of love. I would not miss this chance to be with my family in a way I knew I could, unlike when I became a first-time parent.

Julia was free to be picked up and held. The cords monitoring her condition provided enough length that I could prop her up in my arms, supported by a soft pillow. We glided together in the rocking chair for over two hours. I marveled at her innocence, beauty, and acceptance of my tender touch. She bestowed comfort upon me as she received my soft, delicate touch and soothing voice. She opened her eyes briefly to see me giving her so much loving. I whispered, “It’s me, Julia. It’s Daddy.”

We soon realized the sunlight and glare from the neighboring window were too much for her delicate eyes. So, we rearranged our little corner space, revealing a sight I will never forget: Julia’s beautiful blue eyes. She and I nestled in endless, uninterrupted staring.

Our gaze connected us to who we each were.

Her bright blue eyes had captured my blue eyes once before, but this time no one else was around. It was just the two of us. I gave to her, and she gave to me. A true give-and-take fostering affirmation; nurturing; tender, gentle touch; and a soft, intimate visibility with a connection unlike anything I have ever experienced.

Chapter 7

A DIFFERENT KIND OF TOUCH

I grew up as one of six children. I was kind of the middle child of the first five kids as we were all so close in age and my youngest brother was twelve years my junior. My sister, the eldest, co-raised him as if he were her own. She also significantly contributed to supporting all of us boys. I do not have many memories before the age of eight, so I can't speak firsthand as to how much love and affection I received of the kind I provided Julia. I am told by my mom, "Of course you did!" I know I was given something somewhere along the line in those early years and for this I am grateful.

Shortly before my thirteenth birthday, I left home with a number of other neighborhood boys to attend a boarding high school seminary to begin my religious formation toward becoming a Catholic priest. The school was located some five hundred miles from the streets of Brooklyn, which was all I knew. It was on these streets and in our brownstone living that I began to first recognize and later in life came to fully appreciate, the messages given me about my family identity and role and what "family membership" entailed. I learned from both my birth family and my religious family that membership has its privileges, as well as serious attached costs.

The privilege of family membership was being branded Dopey Danny, incompetent, despite how "successful" I appeared in the outside world. My role (job) was to do well "out there," but not in the home. The cost to me was always make sure I felt badly about whatever I achieved both in and out of our home. My privilege was to never own what I had achieved. I was to give away my sense of accomplishment, so long as I never got too close to really "owning" my worth.

My cost for living was never to feel good about who I am or could become. One danger attached to questioning my family role (this sense of how I should see and know myself) was the resistance that followed from my family. They fought any alternative version of me from emerging.

They'd remind me, in not-so-subtle ways, that I really wasn't that good, that so-and-so was better than me, or that I should have done better. Even worse than that was how often they seemed to treat me as if I was invisible. It seemed that any deviation away from my family identity, no matter how good it appeared to be for me, meant that I'd have to face the very difficult task of both working against what family membership required, while also struggling to face the challenge of creating a new identity to live on my own terms.

This has been no easy journey. It has felt at times like traveling alone in the desert, sailing in uncharted waters, or orbiting aimlessly among the stars. No matter the metaphor, there I am and so too my family, struggling to find our individual and collective ways.

My relationship with Julia catapulted me into possibilities of relating to myself in new ways both outside my family membership identity and within it. How was I going to take this significant event of my daughter's birth and relate with my family, myself, and Julia? Was it possible to relate in new ways where I could be freer to become who I knew I always could be; who I was intended to be?

***I pleaded,** Julia, please show me the way.*

Chapter 8

A CLOSER LOOK AT A DIFFERENT KIND OF TOUCH

One of the important gifts I received from Julia was a reawakening of my concerns around the issue of touch. My desire to touch and be touched, both physically and emotionally, was finally available to take a closer look at.

My experience of touch with Julia was so different from the kind of touch that gave me a sense of belonging in my family, which had its costs and privileges. Then I entered another family, the seminary, where to belong meant to be abusively taken advantage of and physically touched by other touch-starved boys. Most inappropriate touch I experienced was by those my age, but other touch was by older teens and young men (who knew better). Touching my body and soul had come to mean something dirty, secretive, closeted. It immediately translated into a language I knew all too well: touch equals feeling badly about myself. The message from both the students and priests was, at all costs, keep the closet door closed.

Was this the privilege and cost of membership?

This was the double edge that cut my very fabric during those formative years. The bind that sticks. Did I deserve what happened to me or not? Nothing keeps us stuck better than confusion.

Holding and touching my beloved daughter Julia afforded new healthy sensations of the meaning of "belonging." The conflict raging inside me about who it was I was "supposed" to be swirled its wrath. The family system reminded me of the powerful messages needing to be lived out. I was first and foremost to be overwhelmed by my environment. Second, always show up to do my family role (identity) as Dopey Danny and feeling badly about myself. Third, be the one in the middle willing to sacrifice myself for whatever others around me needed or wanted.

God gave me a family that created plenty to be overwhelmed with. I was both blessed and seemingly cursed with my ability to be in the middle of things, stay there and take it, fight, flee, come back, and thank God: to forget, when necessary, my deep despair and pain. But I also know this journey is about feeling joy, hope, the possibility of life-with-death side-by-side, strengthening me. It is about helping accept my road of recovery—a day at a time.

Entrusted by God to be sensitive to others has had its cost too, namely, me. What about me, God damn it? I gave so much of my life in religious servitude. For what? To be abused? For whom? For everyone else's benefit? I know that isn't the whole story from those years. Good relationships built me up too. I wouldn't be the man I am today without that part of my life, but sometimes the good takeaways are like the road away. This road was filled with negative memories and uncertainty I could never face. Or could I?

Being able to yell and scream isn't new for me. There were many times in my teenage days while alone in chapel, accompanied only by the flickering candles; I knew You heard my lament, confusion, torment, and screams for justice and peace. You felt my pain and despair over how I had been touched. You knew my desire and longing for the loving touch of others and self. You heard me. As I moved along in my seminary training, You provided certain people in my life who provided a safe sanctuary and helped me discern a way forward out of the darkness into the light.

This light was me.

I shined and became more visible to myself and others. I claimed my newly named truth that was both real and being revealed. Guidance for these gifts was provided on this difficult path with Julia, where each unknown became known. Each uncertainty, each scream into the darkness, led to my singular question, "Couldn't her life be spared, allowing her illness to be mine instead?"

The answer was there if I was willing to listen.

Chapter 9

WHAT'S THE PLAN?

Giving away my life is what I learned to do so well, often in the service of self-destruction.

"Don't tell me what to do, damn it!" I defiantly yell out at God or whoever will listen.

"Please, tell me what to do," I desperately inquire, once again experiencing my fearful confusion. The bind that sticks. I know this well.

To be a boy, to be a girl, stuck in a boy's body. Is this strange? Am I strange?

"You're weird!" my brother and his friends back home would assure me on those lonely, brief vacations home among the membership. In addition to being told I was Dopey, I'd get even harsher messages: "You're queer! You're a faggot like all those seminary boys!"

So, in order to counterbalance their harsh, hurtful comments and my abusive experiences, I dated girls while on my summer vacations and Christmas breaks, sometimes two or three girls at a time. This behavior, in fact, was the recommended antidote given me from the director of students, designed to help redress the negative realities of seminary campus life.

He knew what was happening and did nothing to stop it. Instead, his advice on how to deal with it was to swing the pendulum the other way. Date multiple girls during my limited time at home. I guess this was supposedly going to provide the healthy sexual development counterbalance plan I sought.

That's the plan? Go the other way?

While on vacation, I walked home early many an evening because I chose not to hang out with my friends.

My mom would reassure me at the door, "You are special and it is okay to be different."

As an insecure teenager, hearing this from my mother was like receiving the kiss of death, but on the other hand, it was like the comforting glue that binds. She'd invite me to stay close to her so that she could take care of me, teach me and help me navigate my problems. Dad, on the other hand, would encourage me to go and do whatever it was I needed to do and think about taking care of me first. He came right out and told me that I was no longer needed to keep him and my mother together. He'd assure me that they'd be okay without me.

I was so confused! I hadn't told them what really happened to me until many years later. So, I was left to wonder alone. Don't go, stay close by? Go, do your own thing! Stay? Go? What do I do? Go the other way? Which way is that? I've grown up feeling the bind that sticks, to be confused and unsure of myself.

Even now, I wonder what I am talking about. Doubting myself is a running internal tape in my head. I tell myself how worthy I am by how confused I can become. Chaos is my constant companion wherever I go. You tell me what to do, what to think, what to feel. I'm confused, especially about what I want. Yet everyone counts on me to bring clarity to their situation. The bind that sticks. Be confused and be clear.

What does all this talk about being caught up in my parents' relationship, being abused, girls, boys, siblings, and friends have to do with my call to touch Julia and be touched by her and the plan to move forward anyway?

Everything!

Growing up in my family and even to this day, the issue of healthy touch, as I remember, was nearly nonexistent. I half-fondly experienced the obligatory kiss on the cheek offered to my mother upon my greetings and departures. I enjoyed my father's genuine hugs and kisses, except when he was drunk.

I vividly recall what was affectionately referred to as an "Irish touch." "Wait until your father gets home!" was the common threat. I remember anxiously awaiting Dad's arrival home to be hit with his belt. The beating enforced my mother's displeasure with something my brothers or I did. The terror lay not so much in the actual hits, but in not knowing how drunk Dad might be while giving out the beatings. The real fear was not knowing if we would be struck within some limitations or not. Would we receive the leather end or the buckle end of the belt? Did he have any awareness of either, and how much pain he was inflicting?

If it wasn't Dad dishing out the blows, I could count on my older brother striking my mid-back with "the punch," sometimes forcing my two younger brothers to join in taking turns. He often took advantage of my bronchial condition by unprovokedly coming up behind me and punching my upper back and knocking the air out of me. He remained to witness my panic subside as I finally retrieved a full breath. And then, he would deliver the punch, repeating my panic, only stopping once he was bored, I guess. So many times, I experienced being a punching bag as if tolerating it was my indoctrination into the privilege of family membership: take it, don't cry, don't tell or else, take more and just feel badly. The cost—me!

I learned my family value by how many punches and how much pain I could take. My role was to feel badly about myself, despite my stellar performances out on the hard court or ball fields of my youth. My role was to always look for opportunities to mediate family conflict. Communicate for the different parties who hardly communicated with one another and, in fact, hardly communicated with me. I was to somehow know what the other person was feeling, thinking, and wanted communicated. This was my superpower and curse. The most difficult unspoken job I possessed was to remain at home so my siblings could get out of the house while I loyally protected Mom from the return of her often-drunken husband. I was to remain invisible and only be used for their benefit.

Maybe only today can I now more fully appreciate why it was so difficult to remember much of my life story. At the age of twelve, I ran away from home, entering St. Mary's seminary boarding high school to fulfill my role to be the next generation's family priest. My maternal grandfather, multiple great-uncles, and uncles all also attended St. Mary's. Only one among them actually became a priest. I gave up on my aspirations to play in the Major Leagues to become what I thought they needed me to be. It was also difficult to leave my wonderful girlfriend, who never knew why I was really leaving. I said what all the other fellas that were going away said: "I'm following my vocation."

After I departed, the feeling of home followed me and combined with a new kind of teenage touch that hurt in a different way. My new confusion lay in trying to reconcile the dichotomy of both violation and pleasure side-by-side from other young men and boys. My body didn't hurt anymore from my brother's punch or strikes of the belt from Dad. I didn't have to walk home alone anymore. I got away, so I thought, from being in the middle of keeping Mom and Dad together.

Your call, Julia, offers me another view of the possibilities of touch that has little to do with you and much more to do with how I face me, who I am, and who I am becoming. My hope is that there is a softer, gentler side to me that survived and can emerge from those challenging years. Either way, I believe it prepared me well to truly respond to your call that fills me with enhanced freedom of choice to intimately be in relationship with myself and you.

You gaze up at me, your daddy, with your sky-blue eyes for perhaps the final time. I wonder, can you see me? Really see me? Do you know me? What have you to say about how I have cared for you so far? I sit here holding you, struggling to listen to you, to receive from you. Wondering what it is I can give to you and to myself. Can I move away from those strong desires to blame my family for the interference I feel connecting with you and with myself? Can I forgive those whose touch did not take me into account? Can I let go and forgive the bearer of each blow now that we have grown up? Can I move toward greater intimacy appreciating the experiences given me by all those who have touched my life in one form or another?

Julia, you are precious to me.

Thank you for the gift of sharing space, seeing me, and hearing my story. I have known true *presence* holding you in my arms and in the beauty of our eyes meeting. I can more deeply love myself because of our intimate connection these second and third days together, a real, lasting privilege. Now this sounds like a real plan on how to live and love moving forward. I am less scared now.

Chapter 10

DADDY, CAN YOU HEAR ME?

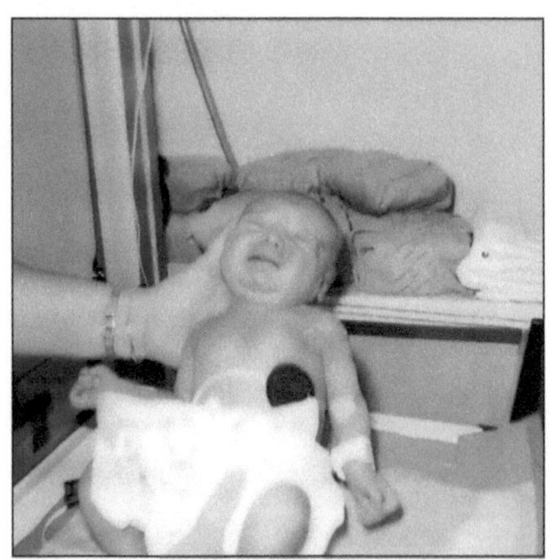

Daddy, can you hear me? Can you feel my love for you? *You seem so busy learning about me, telling everyone about me—stop—slow down and be with me. I'll be leaving soon. While you were home with Kevin and visiting Mommy in her hospital, I overheard the doctor and nurses talk. They found a bed for me in another hospital, some place called Boston Children's. They say I'll have my operation done this morning at ten o'clock. I know it's early, but hurry and catch up with me. I've got so much more I want to say and do with you. I want to jump back into your tender arms again and hear more about that little boy in you that you have been working so hard to heal and love.*

I need some healing.

Hurry back to me and give me some more healing touch—it is so good for me! I wish you were taking the ambulance ride with me. I hope at least I'll have time again to hold and continue looking into you and you into me. They said I would dream while they hold my heart in their hands. It's your heart, though, Daddy, that I'm worried about. You seemed a little uneasy when we last talked. It seemed hard for you to slow down enough to hear my answers to your beautiful questions. Let me try again. I know you're worried about Mommy and Kev too, but I'm worried about you! Can you hear me now? Will you let me love you?

I know it is hard doing all this running around on my account, but Daddy, I want you to know, really know, that I do see you! I do love your gentle voice caressing my spirit, your soft hands stroking my cheeks, your wonderful eyes looking back inside me. Tell me, what do you call those drops flowing out of them? They felt wet.

You talked to me yesterday about wishing you could trade places with me. What does that mean? Did I do something wrong? Don't you want to be my Daddy? I need you to keep giving me YOU! You feed me! Your struggles, your pain, your confusion, your despair; I know these too. It's okay to have these, for they are the flip side of challenge, joy, clarity, and hope. You can't have one without the other. It's like life-and-death. They go together. You need to live both as fully as possible to experience what each has to offer, is the point. So don't rush past either to get to the other side. Be where you are in this moment, knowing you are side-by-side all the time with the other, getting ready to face it even if you are not aware of it at the time. You taught me that, Daddy.

What's a dream? What is my heart?

They say they are keeping a hole open in there to help me pump. Since it's broke, does that mean I'm broken? Can my feelings still work even though my blood isn't flowing inside my heart right?

Hurry, Daddy! I have more questions. I need you! They are starting to put me to sleep. I hope to dream of you, Mommy, and Kev some more.

Chapter 11

WHERE CAN I FIND HER?

"I got here as soon as I could. My daughter is Julia Gene Pender. She has been transferred from Hartford Hospital this morning and is undergoing emergency heart surgery that was scheduled to begin a half-hour ago. Where can I find her?"

"Fourth floor, north wing," the receptionist replied. "Report at the desk and they'll help you."

"I was told that upon arrival here a liaison nurse would update me on her condition."

"I will let her know you have arrived and I am sure she will be out shortly to update you on your daughter's condition."

I only waited about half an hour before the liaison nurse introduced herself to me. She invited me to talk in one of the private rooms equipped with comfortable chairs. She welcomed me, asking if I had any questions. She assured me that no question was trivial. I could not believe how quickly my mind distorted itself, hearing the word "dopey" instead of "trivial." This was a fleeting thought as she again so gently shared her update with me. She was in Julia's surgery the whole time and was well-informed. She helped me understand Julia's current status as though I were actually observing the procedure. Even though I couldn't retain all the technical information, I appreciated her patience with me as I tried to take it all in. She made me feel like I was really present with Julia, as if I were in the operating room caressing her hand and supporting the medical team.

I cried when she told me that Julia's heart stopped once and that her kidneys also temporarily failed. My heart once again went out to Julia, and I wished out loud it were me, not her, in the operating room. The nurse comforted me and spoke of the resiliency of infants to endure, bounce back, and overcome this particular kind of setback. She went on to tell me that the procedure would take at least another hour or so. She encouraged me to take some time for myself.

Imagine that: a perfect stranger knowing that I had raced out of the house, caring for everyone else's needs except my own. She was truly a Godsend. She invited me to nurture myself after my trip of nearly one hundred miles across the state. Come to think of it, this perfect stranger found me to be quite competent and not at all dopey. I truly was in a strange land, so un-family-like. So, I took her advice. I took the pager she offered as well as directions to the cafeteria, along with the assurance she'd page me when any news warranted.

As I walked in the land of unfamiliar hallways and hospital scents, I prayed a short prayer for hope and strength for all involved and gave a mention of thanks for the care rendered to both Julia and myself thus far. I found the cafeteria and later the family and friends waiting area for children in surgery. My pager had not gone off. I found a phone to call Mellon on the western side of the state and pass on what I had learned so far. I then called down south to family in Brooklyn. It was so good getting off the phone and back to the present, where I struck up conversation with some of the other parents. I found this to be very supportive.

Time seemed to stand still, yet passed anxiously. The wait was torture. I just wished time was up and the surgery was completed. Time and nature, however, had their own way. A snail's pace soon leapt into a nail-biting clip as the top-of-the-hour update finally came without any news. I approached the administrator sitting behind the front desk and insisted I be told something, anything. She made a call and told me that the liaison nurse would be with me as soon as possible and that this was all that she could tell me for now. Again, I insisted on an update. Any news, I thought, was better than no news. The update came. Julia had further complications.

Should I have been so insistent, pressuring the administrator as hard as I did? Would it have been easier not to know? Which was better, to know or not to know? Living in the land of the unknown was not an uncommon space for me. I had faced many other moments in my life where I anxiously embraced not knowing. Being in the moment and going through it was familiar territory, but this time it was about my little girl. I didn't know if I could handle this kind of uncertain space, especially alone.

I came to realize that it wasn't just about not knowing the specifics of how and what Julia was experiencing. It was also about not knowing how Mellon, still recuperating herself, was handling the torment of new motherhood without her baby and not knowing what was going on for Kevin during this unsettled separation. Beyond all this was my own anxiety about how I would handle the pending news of Julia's procedure. Ultimately, however, I realized facing the unknown was really about facing me, my role as dispenser of information and the lure to become invisible in this process.

I wanted to know and cease living in the unknown.

Somewhere along this tumultuous journey, however, I came to know that my family-assigned role of invisibility didn't have to rule me. I didn't have to lose myself as the cost of knowing. I grew confident that I could be present visibly in the moment with my needs and feelings with whomever I encountered, especially with family members on both sides.

The liaison nurse finally arrived with news that the procedure was winding down. One of my greatest fears was realized when she told me that Julia's heart had again stopped and her kidneys were compromised, shutting down for a second time. What would all this mean?

I was left holding all this uncertainty.

Chapter 12

OUR FLUID CHILD

The word came that I was finally allowed to see Julia. I hurried to the elevator and made my way to the fifth-floor pediatric intensive care unit. What would I find waiting behind the drawn curtain? After introductions to the nurses caring for Julia, I met with the head pediatric cardiologist for his current assessment. Words were exchanged, but I was already around the curtain holding my baby.

"You can see her now." The doctor startled me from my trance.

I walked into Julia's private room to find her elevated some four feet off the ground on a stable stainless platform bed about 20 by 30 inches. Above her was an extended illuminated roof-like canopy attached to a vertical tower with multiple lights. These lights were like a floating blanket keeping her warm. Along the top of the tower was a thin metal rod with several hooks securing the current IV and dangling medication bags. My Julia was connected to an IV drip, three bags of liquid medication, respiratory tubes, and tiny wired pads. They were scattered all over her body, connected to their own monitor registering each heartbeat, the EKG of life. A glowing red light attached by a brown Band-Aid was connected to her left large toe, measuring her oxygen levels. There was an 8-inch by 1-inch plastic cylinder container hanging over her head funneling the various medication drips down into her through a maze of clear, flowing tubes. Two patches were taped across her eyes, shielding her from the intense brightness of her light blanket. Both of her arms were stretched out and pinned down by her sides.

Beeping, blinking, flashing numbers and graphics registered every breath, pulse, and pressure. All this high-tech equipment filled the shelves behind and beside her. I stood at the foot of Julia's platform table-bed and there it hung: The Bag. This durable 8- by 12-inch bag hung low, almost touching the floor. It had numbers running up its whole side measuring exactly how much fluid was captured coming out as a result of every fluid provided. All I could do was stand in amazement at the complexity of what I was seeing.

The image of Julia as my *fluid child* immediately came to mind. I urgently began trying to reconcile the disconnect between my unplugged little girl I had held just yesterday and the complexity of my fluid child lying on the steel table before me.

I entered this moment. I began to study every drop, every tube's source and ending, and every tube's color nuance. One of two larger tubes was not producing clear fluids. I traced it backward from the top of the bag up to and disappearing under her tiny diaper. I quickly figured out that this was her urine output being stored and meticulously measured in The Bag.

The other larger tube appeared to be attached to her belly. It was a longer, translucent rubbery tube that was thicker than the others. It was pale yellow and very flexible, but its source was disguised by bandages and tape. I could see bubbles and blood droplets within it. As I later came to find out, this tube was still directly attached into Julia's heart somehow. That's why there was a stream of mixed bubbly fluid flowing through it. As I looked further up from her belly, I marveled at the specially designed chest protector covered with a large Ace bandage. It covered from below her neck down to just above her waist. The surgeons intentionally had not closed her chest after surgery in case the need arose to do another emergency procedure. I couldn't believe that under this chest protector was my little girl's beating, malformed, surgically repaired heart.

Her nose was not visible due to all the tape holding the tubes in place. Only the underside of one nostril (the one without a tube in it) could be seen. Her mouth was sagging to the side to which her head was tilted. Her mouth also had a rather large tube that lay between her swollen lips; this tube was attached to an even larger flexible extension hose (the size of a vacuum cleaner) that attached to a machine that was breathing for her.

Her swollen left cheek and ear was all I could see of her delicate face. Her hair, her peach fuzz, was as I left it; slightly blonde with intense shades of red. Her overall complexion was off-white, covered with swollen red patches. Next to her right ear, lying beside her as if an intimate bedfellow, was a sophisticated miniature plumbing network. It displayed multiple color-coded valves and switch stations supporting the delicate combination of measured fluids feeding her fragile body.

I slowly began to move to Julia's right side. I hesitantly approached her as I cautiously passed over and between the wires and tubes so as not to disturb them. I peered under the hooded lights over Julia's body and kissed her forehead.

I tearfully whispered into her ear, "Daddy is here, Sweetheart. I am with you now."

Julia's skin was so warm, nearly pure white, and gave off a high-gloss sheen. The small portions of exposed arm and leg were all chubbier than when I last held her. Between the swelling from the procedure and significant retention of fluids, she already looked the size of a one-month-old child.

I stood there that first day and into the following days, challenged to move beyond the hi-tech equipment, wires, medication cylinders, tubes, bandages, and The Bag back into relationship with my daughter. With the help of God, the staff, and my own yearning for intimacy, I became Julia's daddy again. I was not immobilized by the instruments of life surrounding us.

I observed the routines of the staff: the going in and taking out of the fluids, the countless lab tests, the morning consults with the team of doctors, the lunch and dinner breaks. I wrote down as much information I could to process all the change in numbers and care for my little girl. I took an occasional mid-afternoon nap. I woke to the increase of medication cylinders that changed from 3 to 5. It became clear that all this activity by the medical team was not routine to either them, or me, by any stretch of the imagination. The level of personalized care and individual investment by each twelve-hour shift nurse and the dedication of the doctors was extraordinary.

Chapter 13

MOMMY'S VISIT

SUNDAY—6 DAYS TO GO

The day finally arrived. Mommy was here. Mellon was feeling well enough to travel. Our good friend Steve traveled himself to escort her to Boston. Kevin was again in the care of one of Mellon's good friends, Annie. Kevin insisted that Pinky-the-Bear be a stowaway and be presented to Sis with a kiss to keep her company. Steve's shiny black Lincoln Town Car with its leather trim and luxury sound system provided Mellon with a safe and secure feeling. It allowed her to gain much-needed rest during the nearly two-hour ride east across the Massachusetts Turnpike.

Before I knew it, they had arrived and finally the three of us could be together. We embraced and held one another, clinging to this moment, fearful of the next, as if this were the only moment we might have. The anticipation to reunite Mellon and Julia moved us up the escalator, onto the elevator and to Julia's floor. We walked hand in hand around the various curves, corners, and corridors, finally arriving at the pediatric nursing station.

As I had seen with Mellon on the side of the curtain during Julia's birth, she became very focused. She took deep, cleansing breaths to ready herself to slowly enter Julia's place. This was sacred space, where her presence invited connection and intimate relationship. I had prepared Mellon the best I could for what she would encounter. Julia's swollen body greeted Mommy. Mellon was not distracted by all the trimmings, as she was very familiar with these machines, tubes, and drip bags. They were the same instruments of life that she worked with to support so many as a labor and delivery nurse. She knew her beautiful little girl was present and patiently awaiting her arrival.

Mellon gazed over to Julia's nurse, Paula, seeking approval to move forward. Paula smiled and Mellon navigated the plugs, tubes, and wires gracefully.

I witnessed her whispering, "Mommy is here."

She was now able to reach her little one, without the interference of the plastic casket from the first night that covered Julia for transit. Mellon gave her a kiss on her soft peach fuzz. We introduced Steve to our daughter and he too came into the circle of love. Mellon took up my ritual of caressing and placing lotion on whatever skin was exposed. She told Julia all about Kevin's pride and joy gift, Pinky-the-Bear, and how he wanted Pinky to be with her in lieu of him for now. She remembered to give Kevin's kiss to Little Sis. Pinky proudly sat as Julia's guide and protector at the far right of her head next to the clear cylinders supporting our Fluid Child.

The long day soon came to a close. Mellon and Steve had a long ride home ahead of them. Mellon's heart raced, as did mine. Another separation during a time of desperately needed connection was almost unbearable. So, I made a call back home and spoke with Annie. I expressed my desire to have Mellon remain overnight if she was okay continuing her caretaking of Kevin and if he was comfortable with this request. Both were supportive, but Kevin made it clear that he was looking forward to having Mommy home tomorrow. We put the plan in action; she and Steve would remain overnight and travel back in the morning to have Mellon's stitches removed as scheduled.

The rest of the evening flew by. We each again took turns by Julia's side touching, talking, and even singing our favorite tune: "Fly Me To The Moon," which she had heard us sing many times before. Mellon ended the evening as she did every evening, pumping her breastmilk—what I called "Mommy's vanilla shakes"—one last time for the day. We couldn't wait to share them with Julia! We finally landed in our hotel room. Mellon and I cuddled and fell asleep in the restful presence and touch of one another. Our touch was beautiful and as comforting to each other as I believe it was to our little girl. The little boy and girl in each of us that night experienced the tender, loving touch of being held.

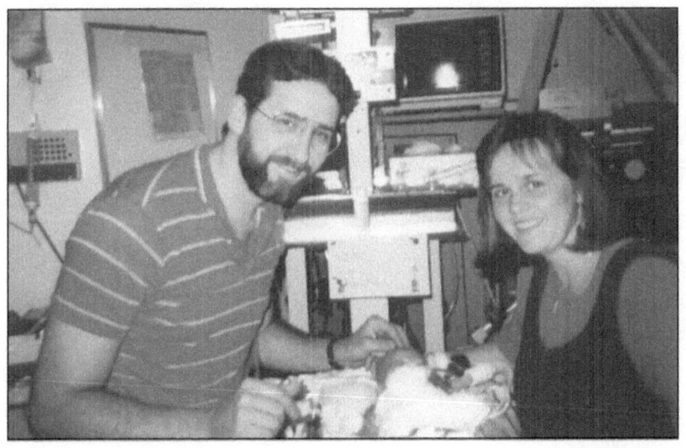

MONDAY—5 DAYS TO GO

After a good, restful sleep, Mellon woke experiencing tenderness in her suture lines, probably due to yesterday's extra activities. After a quick breakfast, we returned refreshed to Julia's place. The overnight report seemed fairly good, yet there was some added concern about her urine output having slowed down. We were aware of this possible complication due to her kidneys being compromised during the surgery; however, it was everyone's hope that full function would bounce back to normal.

Mellon and Steve said their goodbyes despite the uncertainty of Julia's fluid output. Mellon's optimism lingered as we neared our goodbye embrace. We both hoped that it would get better from here. I held onto this optimism as I re-entered Julia's space and watched my baby grow and live another day.

The day progressed. Mellon had reconnected with Kevin and it was now my job to fill her in on the latest doctor meeting. They were more concerned about Julia's decrease in urine output. She was on IV therapy and receiving many different medications via pumps. The toxins were building up in her body. They needed to be released in her urine along with other body fluids. It was decided that in the morning, Julia would return to surgery. The surgeons wanted to check and see if anything from the first procedure contributed to this complication. It was hard for both me and Mellon to sit with this news, especially being separate from one another. We both agreed to grant permission to proceed. Surgery would be scheduled for tomorrow morning sometime.

Chapter 14

BLOW ME A BUBBLE OR TWO

TUESDAY—4 DAYS TO GO

Surgery #2—scheduled for 10 a.m.

My thoughts drift to Kevin before the surgery. I think he's doing well, as best I can tell. He remains plugged into his wonderfully supportive Montessori school program. Child care continues to come from our many diverse resources built over time. A strong network is helping him thrive as Mellon continues her recovery. Kevin's questions are few and his days routine. The other day he wanted to know when his Little Sis would be coming home so that he could hold her again. I didn't know how to answer him, except to say that she was fighting really hard to get better and we were doing everything possible to help. He didn't know yet that her condition had turned for the worse.

The heart shunt bypass appeared to be working perfectly. But maybe not, so they are going in to recheck. Either way, Julia's body is retaining fluid and the numbers are straining all her systems.

What could be causing this? What if anything can fix it? What is wrong? They don't seem to really know, but believe the additional operation is needed to make sure the first procedure was not the cause of the current concerns. Uncertainty colliding with the unknown again. How much more can I take? How much more can my little one take?

I wondered to myself, "Is this all my fault?" Why was this all happening? To me? To my family? I was here and Mellon was there. She'd had to return home to go to her follow-up OB appointment to remove her sutures. Kevin was with yet another caregiver navigating school and being away from his home routine. We hadn't even begun to plan for his fifth birthday party that was less than two weeks away.

Mellon had returned to the place and space where only a week ago she suddenly and terrifyingly experienced the deceleration propelling the urgent need for a cesarean section. I remembered the sheer disappointment of Mellon not being able to deliver vaginally as we had planned and hoped after her first delivery being a C-section.

I recalled Mellon describing to me how Julia was not with her as she should have been at this follow-up OB visit. I had experienced Dr. Kennedy being so attentive and present in every aspect of her practice and delivery. She must have been keenly aware of Julia's absence as Mellon entered the appointment. Mellon shared with me how connected they both were, especially sharing the birthing experience and the few photos snapped capturing the precious moments. Mellon talked about her recent visit with Julia at Boston Children's Hospital and the second surgery scheduled for that morning. The sutures were removed. Instructions were provided, especially to care for the irritated area. Final tears were shared between them. Mellon then updated me about the visit. She was now awaiting my next update call about how the surgery went. I proceeded alone down to the family waiting room. The surgery began on time. This surgery was not as extensive as the first and took about half the time. I waited in the family surgery section as before. Finally, the first surgical liaison nurse update came. She informed me that the original shunt bypass surgery was holding just fine; it wasn't the problem. The problem was Julia's kidneys. Even after the second surgical procedure, the doctors were no closer to determining the initial reason for the first postoperative complications. Julia's kidneys became the focus of her recuperation. The fact that her heart stopped twice during the first procedure led to her kidneys being compromised. At that time, we couldn't tell if having the decrease in circulation to the kidneys would affect their functioning. The doctors described to me how this compromise could be a temporary condition or be core to the eventual shutdown of the kidneys.

Our concern grew.

Prior to re-entering Julia's room, I was informed that this time the doctors had closed and stitched up her chest. Julia's chest was still covered, but this time without the raised chest protector. I found her to be even more bloated than before and showing signs of widespread bruising. The intensity of her overhead light blanket was decreased. The eye patches were removed, revealing how swollen her eyes had become. They remain sealed shut with medicated ointment.

Julia's drip medication cylinders, lined up over her head, now numbered six. The P waves of the heart, which are the waves that measure the normal range of activity, now were measuring on the high end of the desired average range of 125. Our one hope remained that Julia's urine output would increase with the additional medication. Her fluid output was getting dangerously low.

At this point, I recall taking some time for myself to gather my thoughts and feelings about this latest turn of events. I positioned my elevated bar-style stool across the room near the corner window. I moved back and forth between looking out the window, peering down at the people walking the streets, and gazing at my precious bundle over in the other corner of the room. Julia's breathing continued to be artificially supported. Each breath was measured and rhythmic. Her chest would ever so slowly rise and fall with each breath. As I looked over at Julia, I began to notice something unusual happening for the first time. The tiny space between her lips that wasn't taped over to hold the tube in her mouth in place began to give off the most amazing gift—bubbles.

Some of the bubbles were ever so tiny. Over time, they would occasionally cluster, popping freely and unpredictably. Now and again, a rare big one would grow to show off her life. It would pop and another would begin to blow up. Julia was talking to me and I was listening! I reached over and grabbed my notepad and pen. This was our eighth day together. In the privacy and intimacy of the moment, I wrote our poem:

Bubbles

Blow me a bubble or two…
Lift your chest, another time
Peek through your windows to life
and show me your true baby blue colors.

Drain and drip fluid child
Pee just another CC for us.
P waves speak to me of rhythm,

149, 159, 169, – slow down –
the EKG of life shifting…
not too high, not too low.

Little bubbles, pop for Daddy.
Show me your strength of eight long days.
You've been poked and probed,
suctioned and stitched,
opened and finally closed.

Tubes of life handled with care,
nourish me, feed me, as I await
Mommy's vanilla shakes.

Talk about me and help me grow,
grow to live another day,
when my bubbles
can freely blow.

Today
is my challenge
to pump and blow;

Tomorrow
is my dream date…
I hope to go.

Come with me
on my journey so slow;
come, hold my hand as I blow.
Tuesday 5/28/91—Daddy

Imperfectus Interrruptus–I

I'm taking a week off writing my column telling our story of love about the special relationship with our daughter, Julia Gene, to reflect on the process of writing our story, as well as to share some of the readers' feedback I've received up until this point. I almost can't believe over half of the story has already been published. Week after week, I marvel at the story as it unfolds in this column. Even though these first several chapters were written in their original form some three decades ago, I'm struck at how alive the story remains in me today. One of the challenges of writing and modifying this story today has been staying true to my memory of the events as I originally wrote them. Often, I want to editorialize and move away from the original emotion and recollection of the events because they were either so painful or too intimate.

The word "today" is relative because today has taken on new meaning over time. I've allowed myself today, in 2025, to update and expand beyond the original manuscript differently than if Mellon had elected to be involved in this book.

Feedback to my telling our story has been overwhelming. Many people have personally commented that I am very courageous to be writing such a personal story about my experience with Julia, my family, and my personal history as it relates to the story. I've benefited from many others sharing some of their own memories and stories of loved ones who have died. I have been struck by how telling our story has invited healing and new ways of keeping our most important relationships alive, despite death's apparent finality. I am encouraged to keep writing our story, especially at this most difficult juncture in the storytelling. It was no accident that I stopped writing at this very point in the story. With your continued support, I now look forward to the challenge and reward of writing anew the second half of our story of love. Besides, so many people have said they are looking forward to hearing how the story continues. I can't imagine stopping now, despite the ongoing temptation not to enter into the most intimate details that lie ahead, intersecting that fine line between life-and-death side-by-side.

Chapter 15

FACING THE UNKNOWN

WEDNESDAY–3 DAYS TO GO

The bubbles pop, the heart is fixed, the kidneys are shutting down, the dialysis is failing, and the final new medication is our last hope. What is the next unknown that we will have to face? I still cannot wrap my head around a newborn receiving a shunt bypass and now dialysis. Is this even possible?

My heart is hardening. I need help. What is happening to my little girl; my first girl who I was terrified of having? *Give me another boy*, I thought. I knew how to raise a boy. I immediately doubted my ability when I knew I was having a girl. Could I connect the best parts of me with her? So far, so good, I thought. In fact, better than good.

Julia, you bring out the "whole" of me. I am not split. I am capable of being present with you despite not knowing what's next. Who ever really knows what's next, anyway? Knowing ahead of time what is in the future is a myth, a fantasy. It is sometimes even a lie we tell ourselves and others to run away from now, from then, from a possible future outcome. I know this to be true especially when the frightening unknown may be the inevitable future.

Mellon and I each prayed and hoped for Julia's full recovery. It seemed clear to me that I was further along than she in the process of considering Julia's probable death. Maybe because this was only her second full day with Julia or because she was just in the beginning phase of the "what if" process. I don't know, but I began hearing some of her doubts, like, "Was this all my fault? If only I didn't have that one drink on the occasion of our sixth wedding anniversary two weeks prior to becoming pregnant. Could I have done something to prevent what happened?"

Mellon was beginning to sound like me. Perhaps my hardening heart propelled me further along into accepting reality. There were now six medication cylinders pumping fluids into our little girl with less coming out despite the dialysis. Was I just too pragmatic? Too insensitive? Too sensitive? Or just facing reality?

Mellon could sense my holding both life-and-death side-by-side. She shared where she was at and how she did not want to talk about her question, "What if she dies?" I was intimately aware and sensitive to this place in her heart for I knew it all too well. I shifted from being terrified of the unknown to what appeared inevitable, even as Julia lay alive in front of us. Life-and-death side-by-side inviting presence.

Together we entered this moment.

Questions began to flow back and forth, mostly logistical, like: How do we keep Kevin in our considerations? Where might we hold the wake? Who might officiate the service? Where would we bury her? What plot size would we select? What kind of service could we create that would both introduce Julia and say goodbye within an evening gathering of so many meeting Julia and one another for the first time? What would communication with each family back in New York look like? I had been the point person each day talking with one key member from each family, our moms. We considered continuing this process of communication with them if Julia died. I would provide the wake and funeral arrangements and request they spread the word to family and friends. Answers to each of our questions came swiftly as we drew upon our intimate connection and how we lived daily.

We held onto hope.

We attempted to remain grounded each day, closely connected in our new intimate reality. We trusted what each day would reveal and how we would meet its challenge, somehow together yet apart.

After this tender, intimate conversation about the uncertainty of tomorrows, I was kissing both my girls good night and goodbye. I was heading back home to be with Kevin and support him tomorrow at his preschool graduation, which would be followed by a picnic. Tomorrow, I looked forward to tomorrow.

THURSDAY—2 DAYS TO GO

It was an ordinary day, with the news that the latest medication and dialysis were not working. As yesterday taught us, time was what remained. How much was unknown. So, Mellon did what she did best—being present with her little girl. The two girls shared their first full day alone together, cherishing the simplicity of being in the moment. What a precious gift given and received. I celebrated my little boy proudly walking the stage to receive his preschool graduation certificate. We played and had fun at the picnic and hung out the rest of the day—finally, some normalcy. We needed normal.

FRIDAY—1 DAY TO GO

Born weighing 5 pounds, 12 ounces, our little girl woke to another day of dialysis not accomplishing what so many were pinning their hopes on. Julia was terribly swollen and bloated from all the fluid retention. Mellon shared with me her longing to finally hold Julia in her arms and wondered if this would ever happen. I got Kevin settled with our very close neighbor friends across the street. Kev was a big fan of them and their dog. He would spend the night with them so I could stay in Boston.

I was back beside my girls by late afternoon. Upon arriving, I quickly assessed how concerning the circumstances for our little girl had turned. Now there were seven medication cylinders and pumps hanging over Julia. Her skin had lost its glow. It seemed stretched to its limit. How much more could her little body expand? Mellon was hoping for a miracle that Julia's fluid output would start increasing.

At eight o'clock we called Kevin to say goodnight. I could immediately tell something was off. Kevin was not his normal confident self. Instead, I could clearly hear his sadness, mixed with what sounded like fear. *What is this?* I thought. *Did something happen?* It didn't matter. What mattered was Kevin being heard when he asked, "Daddy, could you come home and be with me?" Without hesitation, I said goodbye to my girls once again and went to my car, driving across the state in my familiar middle position trying to hold us all together. Despite my exhaustion, I was driven to be reconnected with my little boy.

Chapter 16

IT'S OKAY TO GO

SATURDAY—TODAY IS THE DAY

Mellon was on the phone with me describing that her morning began with receiving the critical news that Julia's condition was failing quickly. She described how Julia's blood pressure had dropped over the past few hours, and only with the aid of an eighth different medication was she stabilized.

Julia was in trouble.

Mellon asked me to come with Kevin as quickly as we could. Kevin, who had overheard the conversation as he nestled up against me in bed before we began our day, was scared. I let him know we needed to grab something quick to eat, hop in the car, and go be with Mom and Sis.

He looked at me and asked, "Is Julia going to be okay?"

I looked back at him and started to cry. So did he. I held him tight, as words couldn't fill the space; only our embrace would give us the strength to get into the car.

"Is Mommy okay?" he muttered.

I assured him, "She is right where she needs to be and we'll soon all be together."

I had just buckled Kevin into his car seat and closed his door when I heard the phone in the kitchen ring again. *I should just get going,* I thought. I didn't want to pick it up. I feared it might be Mellon telling me Julia had died. *Maybe it's best that I don't know who is calling.* I picked up the phone. It was Mellon. Her first words were, "I'm scared." She continued, "I heard Julia's call gently telling me, 'It's okay for me to go, Mommy.'" Mellon assured me she would be okay. Julia was finally in her arms for the first time, tubes and all; another precious moment long awaited.

With tears of sadness in her voice, she said to me, "Honey, I don't know if Julia will make it until you get here. I want you to have a chance to say goodbye to her. I'm placing the phone to her ear now."

I took a deep, cleansing breath and whispered so tenderly and gently, "I love you, Sweetheart. Your heart and love is so strong. You will live in me forever. Thank you for everything you have given me, Kevin, and Mommy. It's okay to go now. Goodbye. I love you."

With that, I hung up the phone, wiping off my tears before going back into the garage to drive across the street to pick up our two neighbors, who were making the trip to support us. We were on our way.

Mellon later told me that right after I hung up, she connected with the nurse, saying, "You don't have to put her through any more. It's okay."

Within minutes, Julia was at peace in Mommy's arms. Julia was free. The two of them sat in the rocking chair for over an hour, finally able to bond. The nurse eventually took Julia to free her from all the tubes, wires, patches, pumps, medications, and machines.

When I arrived with Kevin, the platform bed was bare.

Mellon was in the rocking chair holding our bundle of love in her arms.

We were finally all together.

The reality for Kevin set in without need for words. He hopped onto the rocking chair with Mom and immediately began to hold his Little Sis as he had done before. This time he had a penetrating, blank look on his face. He began sobbing. Mellon and I supported him as best we knew how from each side of the chair. We too began to sob. Kevin had no questions, just presence.

At our request, one of our neighbors took photographs of us holding Julia. One family picture in particular, was striking. It was a picture of us holding one another with Julia's Pinky-the-Bear and Horsy-the-rattle, anxiously smiling for the camera while tears streamed down each of our cheeks.

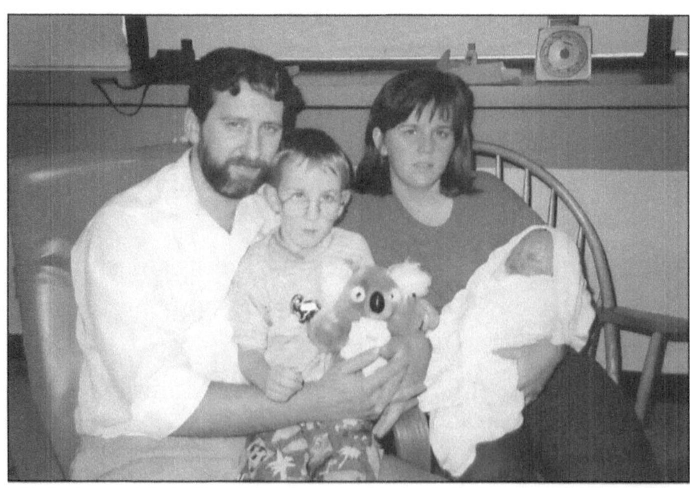

Kevin and I soon unbundled Julia to see more of her. We took in how swollen she had become; multiple bruises were now present. Her skin was visibly stretched out. She still had her beautiful set of reddish-blonde peach fuzz and her skin was so soft, but cold. As conversation eventually started up again, Mellon told me how happy she was that I was able to talk with Julia and how much she thought it comforted her to hear her daddy one final time. We both were struck by the power of that contact and how Julia died only moments after that intimate connection.

Our friends then took Kevin away for a while so Mellon and I could be alone with Julia. We could have sat holding Julia forever.

Forever came too soon.

We decided it would be yet another gift from Julia to authorize an autopsy to help support future research for children with the same anomaly. It was our way of saying thank-you to the team that so deeply cared for our little girl.

We exchanged a tearful goodbye with the staff and thanked them for all their tender holding of our precious little girl. Our journey home was sad and very quiet. We sat in the back seat holding Kevin and one another, deeply connected through the life-and-death side-by-side of the day.

Interruptus – II

The ongoing story of love about life-and-death with our daughter, Julia Gene, will continue in the coming weeks. This week, I want to talk about a column I wrote entitled "Caught in the Middle," prompted by a workshop leader's invitation to describe a real-life dramatic moment depicting understanding of my primary role lived in my family of origin. The purpose of this exercise was to help me name this role I played in my family. This naming is designed to help the individual begin (continue) doing the challenging work of growth, better equip us to move beyond the limits of our family-prescribed role (identity), and more fully claim our potential.

But then there was a twist.

I included this short story in the final draft before publishing my manuscript. However, on the occasion of driving back home after his son's college soccer game, my youngest brother and I found ourselves in an unusual position, alone. I took this unplanned opportunity to tell him my "Caught in the Middle" story since it included him. I didn't know this was his first hearing of this story. It soon thereafter was deemed by my siblings and their partners a forbidden family story to tell and certainly could not be included in my book.

Putting aside for the moment my plan to print this story, what became clear days later was that my brother felt compelled to reveal this story to our siblings and by extension their partners, as well as the news of my pending book publication. He had assured me on the car ride that he would keep that story and my pending publication confidential until I personally disclosed the news to each sibling one-on-one as I had done with him. I soon received word that each sibling recalled that story, was upset that I had told it to our youngest sibling who they believed should have never heard it, didn't want their names used in the story, and felt I should not have read the story to our mother. They made clear in no uncertain terms that this story was *not* to be included in my forthcoming book and that it needed to die.

My ninety-year-old mother's response to hearing me read that same story contained no such demands. Her only request was that I change and soften a few selected words regarding one specific interaction. She was pleased with my immediate edit and fully supported including the revised version in the book. She described to me that her initial response to hearing the story was uncertainty recalling the details of the incident but that she might be blocking it from her memory. She said she believed it happened because of the level of detail I had recalled. She continued, saying how she couldn't or more likely didn't want to remember the incident—despite having interrupted my reading of the story and telling me its ending before I read it. This affirmed the truth of my story and led me to believe my mother at least remembered portions of it, if not the whole incident. Regardless of her full recollection or not, I made the changes she requested.

It didn't matter what I wanted. My family wanted the story killed and my mom supported it being told. Again, I was caught in the middle. So, I informed my family that I had taken that story out of the book. They were pleased. Soon thereafter, when I informed my mom that I had decided not to include that story in my book, I apologized for sharing it with her and thinking it was okay to include in the book. Mom, however, didn't accept my apology. She stated, "You did nothing wrong! It was okay to share that story with me. All I asked was for you to make that one change and you did. It was okay with me for that story to be told in your book and for your siblings to learn from it as you and I have. Your voice is important and I admire your courage to tell this story and I know it will help your readers."

Either way, the point I make telling the above interaction remains the same as the point I made in the deleted story: to name the role I saw myself play in my family. My primary role was to be the one in the middle, be the mediator, the fixer, and most importantly to be caught in this position so as to inevitably lose my self in the service of others and their needs. This was my functional role that I demonstrated in the deleted story. The story was always secondary to seeing myself in it. It always was until it wasn't, when it became more about what everyone else was clearly anxious about—my *truth* being talked about—a family secret becoming public.

I tell the above truth in lieu of the original deleted story to demonstrate my role, which is what remains most important to me. There are dozens of family secrets and stories I could tell if it were my desire to reveal them for their own sake. This of course is not the point of writing my book. Out of love for my siblings, I choose to comply with their demand to make that particular story die by not including it in my book. My dilemma still remains, however, since the deleted story was what my mom had encouraged me to include.

Upon my informing her that I had deleted the story, she understood the bind I was in, stating, "You are caught in the middle." That was enough for me. My functional role after a long dormancy had renewed energy. The point of my role in the middle could not have been better demonstrated than in the differently expressed desires of my family, perhaps even more so than if I had told the original story in its entirety.

Below is the redacted version of "Caught in the Middle." Two different reader responses follow that original publishing.

Caught in the Middle

I was twelve years old…

[column content redacted]

After all, it never really happened, since he couldn't *recall.*

Interruptus – III

Caught in the Middle: Feedback #1

I received this single e-mail response (without signature) to last week's column (6/14/2001) entitled "Caught in the Middle." I am assuming many others who did not respond share a similar reaction. Regardless, I wanted to give this point of view voice. Certainly, I am aware there is part of me that agrees with this point of view wholeheartedly.

Mr. Dan Pender,

I have been a faithful reader of your column Life Through Stories in the Agawam Advertiser News since it began. Lately, I am becoming more and more disappointed with your column. I particularly found last week's column not only distasteful, but disturbing. The timing of this column could not have been worse, right before Father's Day. (Perhaps you planned it that way?) This is a time when we should be emphasizing the more positive sides of our male relationships. I have come to understand, through reading your column, that you had a very difficult childhood, but surely you must have had a male figure in your life that you could have written positively about. A teacher, scout leader, or church figure perhaps? Someone that made a difference in your life for the better. A positive outlook would certainly go farther in helping out more folks who find themselves in the same situation.

Your column seems to be a venue for you to vent your emotional pain and suffering. Some of the stories that you write about should be between you and your therapist as the content is not appropriate to be shared in a small-town newspaper for everyone to read. I believe that the intent of your column was purely for self-help (yours). If you would like to truly help people, please find a more positive way to express and share your stories.

Interruptus – IV

Caught in the Middle – Feedback #2

Last week in this column, I published an e-mail I received from a person describing how he/she experienced my June 14th column and other recent writing as especially "distasteful and disturbing." I wondered with you, who regularly read my column yet didn't respond, if you shared this opinion.

This week, I have given voice to one woman's response, shared by several others this week, that echoes a very different sentiment from the aforementioned individual's feedback. She also directly responds to how she experienced the June 14th column and other writing I've offered. I am aware there is part of me that agrees with this point of view wholeheartedly.

Dear Mr. Pender:

I would like to make a short comment on the article in the *Agawam Advertiser News* of June 21. Like the reader that commented on your articles/writing, I have also been a faithful reader of your column. In fact, this is the main reason for getting this newspaper. I find your writing truthful and fascinating. I look forward to reading the next chapter or column in this paper every week and do *not* find any column "distasteful" or "disturbing"... I have thought of writing to let you know this in the past, but as always, "life" gets in the way and by the time I know it, it's the next week that I think about it, while reading your next article.

Whatever your reasons are for writing this column, I for one find them to be very soul-searching. Not everyone that reads this paper (or as in life in general) has had a perfect childhood, but until being able to "Talk About It," do not know that they are not alone. I think your column is very helpful for them. After all, isn't the current title of your column *LIFE Through Stories...?*

My main reason for writing to you today is the opening paragraph in which you say you "are assuming many others who did not respond share a similar reaction." I just would like you to know that I *do not* share this person's opinion and hopefully you will continue to share your stories with all of the readers of this newspaper. In fact, maybe you should think about writing for larger newspapers or maybe even your own book.

Thank you for letting me vent today and please continue with your own style of writing.

Sincerely,
Mary Schlage

Chapter 17

OUR TEARS, OUR BUBBLES

DAY 1—SATURDAY

After the autopsy back at Boston Children's Hospital, Julia would be transported back to our local funeral home Monday morning. Our ride back across the state without our daughter (and Sis) was the longest of all my rides over the past twelve days and the quietest. What was left to say? I think all our collective tears were cried for now. Our arrival home was next and we knew it was going to be very difficult.

It was.

Our little boy filled the space with life even more than we imagined with everything we had gone through. Kevin was glad to be home and in the comfort of his action figures greeting him. He was soon engaged. But even he could tell something was missing.

Something just wasn't right.

Hesitancy and fear were in the air as we considered going upstairs into Julia's room to experience her space.

The crib, once her big brother's, was all ready to snuggle her. It was positioned just to the left of the twin bed. The closet was filled with gifts and clothes for her to enjoy. The rocking chair nestled in the corner invited the evening feedings, storytelling, and sweet songs. The changing table was stocked and ready to provide a safe and comforting view of the backyard trees and clouds.

It was as it should be but not complete. Julia was there but missing. Mellon, Kevin, and I soon shared her space, quietly at first. Then we cuddled together on the twin bed. Our tears once again spoke for us.

Our Tears Were Our Bubbles.

Conversation finally emerged. Mellon described how her midnight feedings would never be. She wondered aloud, "What will happen next? How can I live without Julia in my life?" These were shared questions that, once spoken, allowed Julia to once again be present in the room, guiding our way forward. She found her way home and we found her—the gift still giving. Our hesitancy and confusion were replaced with clarity.

The message from some family members was to move on, as if it never really happened. Pack up her things and get back to what matters. We did the opposite, because Julia's life mattered. Mellon mattered. Kevin mattered. I mattered. We mattered. Our family's present moment mattered.

We knew this story would shape our future as it has our past. Here, now, and forever is where the past, present, and future co-exist in these precious moments. The Hebrew people called this co-existing moment *El Olam*, which translates to "Everlasting God" or

"Presence" and means "for a long time, always, then, now, and forever present." The experience of time, of being in the moment, was learned through intimate relationship with Julia; where all tenses—past, present, and future—are inescapably *now*. She is present now, thirty-four years later, as she was in my hours and days holding her. A truth from which I write this day.

After our precious time together in Julia's space, it was time to plan her celebration of life. We had a late afternoon appointment at the funeral home. Kevin stayed with neighbors while Mellon and I planned for our little girl's memorial celebration and burial service. Questions of uncertainty arose despite our having an initial outline of a plan. None of this felt right. The thought of even meeting to finalize a wake and burial plan was unfathomable. All I knew was that by talking about it, it became more real, answers became closer, and more questions emerged. What was God's purpose for all this? How would we grow through it? How would we support one another in the unknown moments ahead? We knew one thing for certain: we wanted to create an inviting space to both introduce and say goodbye to Julia.

We all need a space and time for the grief we hold.

The funeral director was very accommodating to meet with us on a late Saturday evening. He began by sharing his condolences for our loss. He then asked if we would like to see the room options for where the memorial celebration would be held. We selected a room, making our first of many decisions. We listened to his presentation about how he thought the wake might function best for us and our guests. He proposed everything, including seating, flower arrangements, furniture layout, and why the casket should remain closed. I asked him for some time alone so we could imagine how we'd like to plan the evening. After some twenty minutes, we invited him back into the room.

I began by informing him that we had made some decisions.

I told him we wanted the casket to remain open. He immediately repeated his concern about our choice, citing from his experience about how difficult this would likely be, not only for us, but for our guests. We listened and moved forward. Next, I informed him that we did not want to place the casket in his recommended traditional location. We wanted it to face out kitty-corner just to the left of the double doors entering the room. He stated his objections to this. I described how we wanted the seating arrangement to be in a semicircle facing the casket with no center aisle. I wanted only one couch to be located to the right of the casket and for all the other couches and tall, straight-back comfortable chairs to line the back walls. His objections grew. Finally, I informed him that we did not want any piped-in music, as he had also earlier recommended. We were going to bring a boom box to play our own music. I continued. We wanted no overhead lights, only one tall, freestanding lamp to be placed between the corner walls and the casket. We wanted it to be on the lowest setting to soften Julia's corner. We also wanted two additional lamps in the room, for a total of five. By this time, the funeral director backed down from expressing his objections and moved to comply with our vision.

We worked out the final details for our Monday evening gathering and preparation for the burial site. We also informed him that we would be inviting our own minister to lead the memorial service. We agreed on three hours for the viewing, with no public afternoon hours. He informed us that the room would be ready by two o'clock for private viewing by the immediate family. He went on to tell us that once we decided if we would have an after-burial meal, he would be the contact person for communicating this and all hotel options in the area for our guests. As we readied to leave, I informed him that our families were all traveling up from New York City Monday afternoon and that only Mellon, Kevin, and I would be stopping in during the late afternoon. I felt grateful for his flexibility and support of our plans for the evening. I left feeling good about the design I had basically created, with Mellon's support, hoping it would invite and provide a space for intimate relationships.

Chapter 18

A DAY OF REST

DAY 2—SUNDAY

Sunday was a restful day of sorts. Kevin woke with the excitement of Christmas morning, having both Mom and Dad home and to himself. He was so looking forward to planning his fifth birthday party that was just around the corner. He had so many ideas and names of friends he wanted to invite. He couldn't be contained and he wasn't. We spent much of the day pulling together plans for his party.

A *birthday party* and a *wake*; two occasions not meant to be planned side-by-side. The cruelty of life-and-death.

Mellon and Kevin went to the nursery and bought marigolds and impatiens flowers to plant. They started around the mailbox, ending with the two flower boxes on our front porch, which had a two-person rocking chair. I sat there, enjoying watching them plant together. After they cleaned up, Mellon shared a great idea to put all the Polaroids from our hospital visits together with our own camera photos. We'd use a one-hour developing location and create a photo album to share with everyone at the wake tomorrow.

Kevin asked, "Can I help?"

"Of course, we can't do it without you," I said.

He smiled and made our day.

Chapter 19

WHAT TO WEAR?

DAY 3—MONDAY

Through the magic of one-hour developing, we were soon putting the prints into our new floral bound three-ring photo album. The story of love, of our family's journey together, would be visible to everyone. The album took shape as the story did. At first it was just random Polaroids, but soon it began to naturally tell the real-time sequenced journey, beginning with Julia's ultra-sound strips, Mom nesting, the delivery, Pinky-the-Bear with big brother Kevin cuddling Sis all nestled in Dad's arms, Julia's head in the oxygen case before her first transfer, her stay in both Hartford and Boston Children's hospital, and more. Calmly putting together Julia's photo story helped steady our mounting anxiousness as we prepared for what we knew would challenge us this evening. We would be sharing our little girl, in effect reliving many of those precious moments, but this time while both introducing her and saying goodbye.

"What am I going to wear?" Mellon wondered. I had already

selected comfortable casual shoes, a pair of dress slacks, and a white shirt with small red stripes with no tie or sports jacket. Mellon, hearing my plan, felt supported to move away from the social expectation she was feeling to wear the obligatory black outfit.

She told me, "My choice was more in line with my sense of self—casual and comfortable." So, for the evening service she chose to wear a comfortable, cream-colored dress she had worn once to a wedding and for Sunday worship. For the burial site service, she did a quick shopping trip and found a blue-and-white striped casual dress that was "her." I was glad she would be comfortable. We certainly expected to feel enough discomfort over the course of the evening.

Kevin's preparation was simple. We encouraged him, as we regularly did within limits, to select what he wanted to wear for the day. On this day, we didn't impose limits on how he put his outfit together. We weren't surprised by what he decided. He came out of his room wearing his long-sleeved white Batman pajama top covered by a light purple short-sleeved T-shirt; a light blue Mickey Mouse hat; dark purple pants with light pink, white, and blue geometric designs; white socks; and his square-shaped, multicolored slip-on sneakers. His special request, which we fully supported, was to create his signature battle-ready Wolverine-style "adamantium" claws using masking tape to attach two washable, colored Crayola markers to each wrist. Kevin's imagination was ready for anything. He never knew when he might encounter an alien attack. After all, he didn't know what to expect tonight. He had his Crayola counterattack at the ready or for a quick sketch to pass the time. This was our Kevin Edward in true form.

We made one final stop at the flower shop before arriving for the private evening calling hours at the funeral home. Mellon ran into the store to purchase a simple, single short-stemmed pink rose with baby's breath. A few minutes later, she hurried back to the car without the flowers. I put the window down to hear what she had to say.

She peeked her head in and asked, "What do you want to put on the card?"

I turned to Kevin in the back seat and asked him what he would like to say to his Little Sis on a card.

Without a moment's hesitation he responded,

"You'll be with us, and we'll be with you always!"

Interruptus – V

Staying in the Goodness

Have you ever been close to something so good that you'd do almost anything to move away from claiming it? I have! This past week has been a case in point. For those of you who have not been following this column each week, I have been sharing portions of a larger story of love about my second child, Julia Gene, who died some ten years ago as of this writing. The challenge each week is writing this story in chapter form to accomplish publishing a book in newsprint. I share this story with you as part of an ongoing process of grieving, healing, and celebrating Julia Gene and our family's life.

Writing and sharing this story has been a process both difficult and joyous. I recently received an e-mail supporting my effort and praising my courage to share such an intimate story. The person went on to say how courageous it also is to expose my and Mellon's marital relationship in public. I agree. I also need to clarify something for this person and for you. Their presumption was that I was simply sharing an already completed manuscript. This was not the case. It was a work in progress.

While I wrote the first six chapters some six or so years ago, closer to the time of Julia's life, this second half of the book takes shape, literally, each week and subsequently many years later in my newspaper column. As mentioned earlier in the preface of the book, the loss of Mary Ellen's direct contribution to this current book-writing process is missed. Her participation was a gift to the original partnership in the newspaper edition. It was a dual opportunity to circle our shared notes, memories, and individual experiences and retell them together.

On this topic of staying in the goodness, I recall this period of time in the writing process was particularly busy for both Mellon and I, but not unlike most. We were about to begin the second half of the story of love. As was our pattern, early in the week we would collaborate on where we had left off in the story, what would come next, and where each of us might put our focus during the week. We'd then come together, usually on Sunday, to see how we might give shape to our reflections. Perhaps due to our three children being home for school vacation and preparations underway to celebrate our soon-to-be one-year-old's birthday, life caught up to us.

The challenge for me this evening, as I press on to meet the morning publication deadline, was to decide if the story was sufficiently ready to move forward. Many things come into consideration. Tonight, we talked and realized a number of things. First, how much we missed our Sunday debriefing time. Second, how much our thoughts and hearts about Monday – DAY 3 were filled with the events of the wake service and how the reality set in that we had finally reached this most important point in the story. Third, we each realized how challenging this portion of the story continues to be, even these many years later. And fourth, I became aware of how very good this experience was for us and those who experienced it with us.

I began to question the "coincidence" surrounding the intensity of work for each of us that week and how it contributed to the overall hectic pace. It was helping each of us move away from writing what we knew would be good for us despite knowing how difficult it would be, in effect, to relive. Perhaps I should just write something unrelated to meet the publishing deadline? I realized that I wasn't ready to move forward under these circumstances.

Interestingly, Mellon came to me independently, stating that she was not ready to move forward writing the next installment of the story either. I shared my sentiments and we collectively shared a moment of relaxation. We realized it wasn't that we didn't want to claim the goodness; it was simply that we weren't ready to share it at this time. We were both in a similar state. Her question followed: "Why not write about our process?" I told her, "I was thinking the same thing!" So, I thought I'd just write a quick paragraph or two this evening. Well, I guess I had more to say than I thought.

Ultimately, I get back to one of the most important questions I ask myself these days, namely, "Am I able to stay in the goodness of the moment or am I running from it?" Tonight, I know I'm not running from goodness. I am sharing our process with you and this is good. I look forward to this week's offering of goodness in the form of having more time to care for ourselves and the ongoing process of claiming our relationship with Julia Gene.

I better hurry up and save this document before the possibility of it inadvertently vanishing into cyberspace and not being published.

That would not be good.

Chapter 20

MOVING ON WITHOUT KNOWING

The story of love continues with a very difficult conversation, as I recall, that Mellon and I had the afternoon of Julia's death back at our home. For the past two weeks, Mellon and I had agreed that I would be the conduit between both our families, to painstakingly inform them of Julia's condition and how we were doing. I kept Mellon in touch with what I had communicated to them and what they had asked me to discuss with her. Despite their desire to directly connect with Mellon, both families respected this arrangement, or so I thought. This put some additional pressure on me as I supported Mellon's need to rest and heal without having to handle both families.

Each family resided in Brooklyn, New York, some ten blocks or so away from one another. My family lived on the one side of the highway in Sunset Park, whereas Mellon's family lived on the other, more affluent side, in a neighborhood known as Bay Ridge. Mellon's immediate family had thirteen members and mine had eight. With such a large cast and facing the difficult challenge of our current circumstances, Mellon and I agreed to limit my contact with the two families during these weeks to two people: her and my mom.

Each day since the birth, I had called Mary (Mellon's mom) and my mom Sheila at least once a day. The climax, of course, was when I contacted each of them Saturday morning to reveal that Julia had died. On Sunday's call, I informed each of them of the preliminary plans that there would be common viewing hours Monday evening with a brief memorial service. Tuesday morning would be the burial service, followed by a meal at a local restaurant. I provided the funeral director's contact information to allow family to contact him for the final arrangements and hotel options in the immediate area.

By midday Sunday, I had heard back from my mom that all but one of my brothers and their partners were going to attend. My grandmother, several uncles, cousins, and aunt would also be attending. I even received a sensitive call inquiring if my sister and aunt could bring their newborns. We wholeheartedly accepted and welcomed their presence.

We had not, however, heard from Mellon's family about their plans to attend. Mellon called Paul, one of her older brothers living in Philadelphia. To her surprise, he had not heard of our daily updates through their mom, nor, most importantly, news of Julia's death and our subsequent plans. He was very upset with his mom for not sharing our news as we requested and she agreed. He called back shortly after a conversation with her to inform us that his mom had not told the other siblings of our daily updates, news of Julia's death, nor our invitation to participate in the memorial service. Paul informed us that he would not be able to pick up his two sisters, who also wanted to come, until very early Tuesday morning. They would drive up to attend the burial service. We were very happy to hear this and felt disappointed that no other siblings contacted or came to be with us. We were also very sad that Mary would not be with us for the memorial and burial service.

We couldn't understand why Mary chose not to tell anyone our daily updates or at least let us know that she would have been more comfortable if we informed everyone ourselves. Perhaps Mary had kept this quiet, as she had wanted her daughter Mellon to do the same.

We would go on with our days not knowing.

Chapter 21

AN INTIMATE GATHERING

DAY 3—MONDAY EVENING

Upon our arrival at the funeral home early Monday evening, the director greeted us at the door and escorted me, Mellon, and Kevin toward Julia. The room was arranged just as we had requested. We thanked him for his efforts and informed him of our desire to have some private time. He reassured us that everything was ready for our guests for this evening's viewing hours.

We anxiously approached Julia.

Kevin carried our single pink rose as he slowly walked alongside Mellon. Mellon carried, along with her pocketbook, a small bag, its contents unknown to me. I moved toward the two-person kneeler located just in front of Julia. Kevin, in his usual playful manner, ran ahead of us to see his Little Sis. He jumped up on the kneeler and stood leaning over the rail, head-to-head with Little Sis. Julia was dressed in a soft white, long-sleeved shirt trimmed with mint green. It buttoned up on the right side. A soft mint-green pair of pants and blue booties covered her swollen legs and feet. Despite Julia doubling her original body weight, the outfit, which had been gifted by Mellon's co-worker and friend, fit perfectly.

The blue booties were imprinted with the saying:

I Love Daddy.

Julia appeared cozy in her little cradle-like white coffin, even with the heavy makeup covering cheeks that were bruised from her long, hard journey. Her head was covered by her white cotton cap, adorned with a fluffy pink pompom. It read "I'm from the Family Birthplace at Providence Hospital."

I recall Mellon saying, "What a comfort it is to finally see our little girl at peace without all the tubes and bandages. She is so beautiful in her first outfit."

Kevin gently removed Julia's cap as if trying not to wake her. He stroked her wavy, reddish-blonde (towhead) hair.

"She's cold!" he whispered.

"Yes, she is," I replied, as I leaned over him to stroke her forehead.

Mellon leaned over and held Julia's left hand. We remained in silence for a precious few moments, touching Julia separately, yet as one. Mellon reached into her bag (Julia's luggage) and pulled out Pinky-the-Bear and Horsy, the yellow-and-white rattle. She placed Pinky at Julia's feet and Horsy on her pillow next to her left cheek.

We were all reunited again.

Chapter 22

GETTING TO KNOW YOU

Before we opened the double doors to allow our guests from New York, our town, and our places of work to enter into Julia's and our space, Mellon and I talked separately from Kevin. Mellon said it out loud: "I feel profoundly inadequate and scared. This is our little girl. How am I supposed to be? How am I supposed to act?" She further described to me the pressure she felt to act normal in a situation that wasn't normal.

There is nothing normal about burying your child.

Mellon was asking important questions on topics we hadn't talked about. We took these final few moments to review how we had discussed in detail the seating plans, music, lighting, scripture readings, and even my talk, but had not discussed how to cope with what was right in front of us.

I looked at her and said, "We'll figure it out as we go. Let's start by standing at the door greeting everyone as they enter and let the rest play out naturally."

She agreed.

I opened the double doors.

We took this moment as our first real opportunity of the evening to personally welcome everyone and thank them for coming. Of course it was very awkward meeting under these circumstances, but it helped make this first transition of the evening go very smoothly. Kevin, without prompting, found his special way of participating. He soon left our side and very spontaneously jumped onto the kneeler and proudly stood by his Little Sis. I glanced over with admiration on more than one occasion, seeing him introduce Julia to our guests. As each person filed by his Little Sis, he encouraged them to touch Julia as he was able to do. He did this so lovingly, proudly, and tenderly. Kevin was being Kevin. He set the desired tone for all to receive our invitation for real intimacy this evening. Everyone settled into the room. It soon became clear it was standing room only. So many people were touched by Julia's life and came to support us. Many came tonight to say "hello" for the first time and all to say "goodbye."

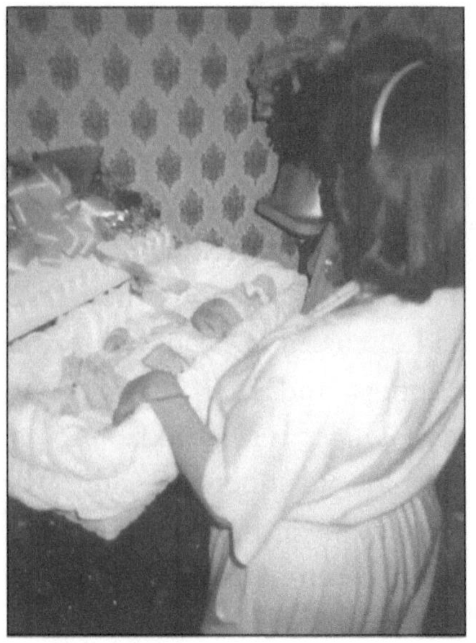

Mellon and I were the last to take our seats on the single couch to the right of Julia. Before sitting down with me, Mellon moved to the kneeler to take a moment with her little girl before we started the service. For me, however, the service had begun with mother and daughter peacefully connecting at last.

This was just another precious moment seared into my heart and mind. My friend

Tom captured the evening's intimate, precious moments on videotape. He immediately jumped into action, peering over Mellon's shoulder and capturing her gaze. Memories are so hard to hold onto, but images like this endure. I soaked up this connection of mother and daughter.

Mellon described to me after everyone left that when she was about to depart the kneeler to move over to the couch with Kevin and me, she had an unbelievable urge to pick Julia up and hold her. She recalled how she suddenly froze, worrying about everyone looking at her and what they might think. All she wanted to do in that moment was hold her little girl one last time, but then decided that maybe she'd just do it after everyone left for the evening. I was struck by her honesty of desire, as I wanted the same thing, without having the courage to say it out loud as she had done.

This was Mellon at her best.

Mellon took her seat on the extra-long couch that could easily seat five. To her right sat my older brother, James. Kevin hopped onto Mellon's lap just to my left. We faced the chairs filled with our guests. I looked out and absorbed the faces of all my family in attendance along with its two newest members, one newborn niece and another newborn cousin. Mellon didn't have her own family faces present to support her as she had hoped. She instead soaked up the love and support that did show.

Mellon trusted my talents to create the intimate space and environment of the evening. She described to me how she felt as though she had hit that point where she just couldn't do anymore. I understood this. I was concerned that one or both of us might succumb, in this moment, to living out our family "role" of her being "inadequate" with "nothing to contribute" and me being "dopey" and "lacking common sense."

I experienced Mellon as an extraordinary woman of tremendous skill, abundant tenderness, empathy, willingness, and ability to provide positive contributions. Tonight was no different. She far exceeded her restrictive family identity, as was abundantly illustrated by her deeply intimate presence and displaying all of the above attributes with Kevin, Julia, me, and our guests. She was hurting emotionally and still physically healing. But her family's message of inadequacy simply had no place here in Julia's and our space tonight. We both had our uncertainties planning for this evening, yet as it started, there was one thing we each held confidently to our core: I was not "Dopey Danny," nor was Mellon "inadequate."

We didn't know how the evening would unfold because there was no script, just an outline, a feel, an intentional desire for intimacy to unfold. This uncertainty was okay. It was finally time to make connections with ourselves and those who had gathered to affirm Julia's life. We desperately yearned to share our experience with our little girl and Sis with our gathered guests.

I got up and closed the double doors.

I invited folks closest to the floor lamps to shut them off. The tall, thin lamp placed behind Julia was the only lamp left dimly lit. I then lit two candles placed on a stand positioned to the left of Julia and to the right of the podium. Our portable sound system was on a small table below the candles.

I introduced Kyle McGraw, our invited guest, friend, and

Methodist minister. He led us in prayer. Kyle spoke openly and passionately about the challenge of connecting with God during this difficult time of grief we held in our hands. He assured us that God's grace was available to all during this time when death-and-life stood side-by-side. He prayed that we find trust in God's goodness and mercy. He led us in praying the 23rd Psalm. He reminded us of what the prophet John wrote in the book of Revelation; namely, that Julia was a child of God and was now in the new Jerusalem. These were comforting sentiments that we deeply appreciated.

I then walked up to the podium.

I was both nervous and unusually calm as I entered into the uncertainty of this moment. I began sharing our story of love and journey with Julia, recounting:

...how we entered the doctor's office and found out that Mellon's cervix was four or five centimeters dilated;

...the anticipation of proceeding directly to the labor and delivery room;

...the longing to attempt a vaginal birth after having had a cesarean section with Kevin;

...the fear experienced from the major deceleration of Julia's heart after the pitocin medication kicked in;

...the anxious move to surgery for an emergency C-section and the disappointment of Mellon not being able to deliver vaginally;

...the terror of a poor APGAR and the delight of Julia's strong comeback;

...the precious first two-and-a-half hours of Julia's life with Kevin, Mellon, and me.

I continued by describing our experience as a roller coaster ride. First, the news came from the nursery that Julia was turning blue and with it, the preliminary diagnosis of a heart problem. Second, the details of Julia needing medication to keep open a heart valve that normally closes three or so hours after birth. Third, how we had to move Julia to Hartford Hospital where the medication would keep her heart valve opened while we awaited a pediatric heart surgeon to become available to execute this delicate surgery.

A bed finally opened up at Boston Children's Hospital and off she went. I followed her as she immediately went into open heart surgery. Both her heart and kidneys stopped and were revived. Julia struggled for the next five days to pass urine. Her kidneys were failing, and a second surgery was performed. The doctors found no damage to the original shunt bypass nor any other possible causes for the kidney malfunction. Her kidneys again stopped and started during this procedure.

The doctors increased her medications to help her fluid production and stabilize her blood pressure (P-waves). They started kidney dialysis.

I then described how, on her eighth day of life, I was sitting by the hospital window writing in my journal when I captured a precious moment. Julia's mouth was taped over to secure a feeding tube. However, a tiny uncovered corner spoke to me.

A poem emerged within me that I swiftly captured.

I was ready to recite it, but as the title of the poem, "Bubbles," came across my lips, I began to weep uncontrollably. I could not catch my breath. I could not continue.

I stood crying at the podium alone for what felt like an eternity. Then, out of the corner of my eye, I saw Kevin spontaneously leap out of Mellon's lap and run past Julia. I bent over to receive him flying into my outstretched arms and wrapping his legs around my waist. He gently placed his left cheek against mine. Mellon arrived just a moment later, putting her arm around me, literally holding me up. As the three of us connected, I found their bond infused me with the strength to continue reading:

Bubbles

Blow me a bubble or two…
Lift your chest, another time
Peek through your windows to life
and show me your true baby blue colors.

Drain and drip fluid child
Pee just another CC for us.
P waves speak to me of rhythm,
149, 159, 169, – slow down –
the EKG of life shifting…
not too high, not too low.

Little bubbles, pop for Daddy.
Show me your strength of eight long days.
You've been poked and probed,
suctioned and stitched,
opened and finally closed.

Tubes of life handled with care,
nourish me, feed me, as I await
Mommy's vanilla shakes.

Talk about me and help me grow,
grow to live another day,
when my bubbles can freely blow.

Today is my challenge
to pump and blow;
Tomorrow is my dream date…
I hope to go.

Come with me
on my journey so slow;
come, hold my hand as I blow.

Tuesday 5/28/91—Daddy

I stood at the podium catching my breath as Mellon's and Kevin's hold continued supporting my stance. I gathered myself and informed everyone that over the next twelve minutes I would play a special piece of music that invited reflection of Julia, our special relationship, and their own personal journey. I described how this piece of music had been a part of my connection with Julia, as I played it over and over while traveling to and from her bedside. The music was from the motion picture *Heart and Souls*. It was ironic that the title of my favorite instrumental track was "Julia's Farewell." I shared my experience of how the music powerfully depicted the peaks and valleys of Julia's and our journey. It portrayed pure exhilaration and joy as well as utter despair and sadness. It captured the intimacy of life-and-death side-by-side. I asked everyone to listen to this inspiring, passionate piece of music and be in-the-moment experiencing whatever it offered.

Mellon took her seat on the couch to the right of Julia. My

older brother James sat to her right as Kevin hopped into her lap. I hit the play button, then sat on the couch, leaving an open space to my left. Kevin wiggled over into my lap. We cuddled together as the music began and so did the magic of the moment. You could hear a pin drop as the trumpets pierced the room. The first movement was riveting. Mellon had a half-filled box of Junior Mints candy that Kevin made his way into. As the tone shifted to capture the sadness of the moment, Kevin dropped the box onto the couch to my left and wiggled out of my lap. He did what many in the room may have wanted to do. He slowly walked over to the kneeler, hopped up, touched Julia and stood there a few precious moments crying. He returned to Mellon's arms and they embraced. His body melted into hers as the music fell to a whisper. Kevin's sobs filled this sacred space.

You could see tears beginning to flow. There was a quiet pause just before the final movement. Just then, my two-month-old cousin, Laura (sitting in the first row with my seventy-seven-year-old grandmother), began to cry. The juxtaposition of life-and-death side-by-side was formidable. As quickly as she began to cry, she quieted as the trumpet fanfare reappeared. My youngest brother, Michael (twenty years old), took this opportunity to move from across the room to sit next to me. He gently placed his arm around my shoulders, touching me like I had never been touched. He tenderly stroked my neck. I placed my left hand upon his right knee, and we shared tears together.

The music concluded.

I allowed a few moments for shared grief and tears. I continued to speak from my seat. I requested anyone to spontaneously offer up (out loud or in silence) a prayer from their heart. My seminarian classmate Tom shared first. Then a friend, Paul, shared. To my surprise, my older brother James was next. This was the first time

I had ever witnessed him pray. He prayed for Mellon, Kevin, and me, asking God to give us the strength to handle this loss and be able to live the goodness that was still ours to have. Just after this, my outstretched arm around Mellon leaned just a bit further to stroke James's neck. He raised his right hand, not to punch me, but to embrace and squeeze my hand ever so gently. In that moment, all the pain and anger I harbored toward him through much of my childhood was healed through the power of genuine loving touch.

The long silence was broken with a final spoken prayer from another unlikely source, my father. Like my experience of James, I had never witnessed my dad praying out loud. His prayer was heartfelt, filled with tears, and deeply moving. He prayed for us to be able to get through our pain during this time and for my family to someday hold joy in our grief.

The silence remained until I invited another seminarian friend, Owen, to play his guitar and sing a song by David Haas entitled "Come and Journey with Me." What a gift this song was for us. I concluded this part of the evening by inviting everyone to pray together the Lord's Prayer. Many reached out to hold one another's hands. Mellon took a few moments, on behalf of me, Kevin, and Julia, to thank everyone for their support and coming to be with us. I stood up and put the overhead lights on and played some soft instrumental music.

An informal greeting line appeared. Hugs were exchanged. Many stopped by Julia and touched her before exiting. This next unplanned half-hour or so was very special. Most friends had departed, leaving my immediate and extended family to visit with one another. My mom and dad made beautiful connections with Kevin. Kevin was so cool hanging out with his great-grandmother, aunts, uncles, and cousins. Like a parched sponge, I absorbed the love offered that was so unfamiliar. I took great pleasure receiving and giving the kinds of love that I had always longed for in my family. It was finally here. It was real and celebrated. This was another one of Julia's many gifts to me.

Both Mellon and I were visible to our family and friends during this celebration of life and heartbreak of death. Being seen was both a vulnerable position to be in and one that was unfamiliar to me in my family. Tonight's joy was accepting their care, concern, hugs, acknowledgement, and love that substantiated what we had hoped for—intimate relationships. This type of visibility validated the opposite of what I understood as Mellon's family system message that she should have kept things quiet rather than make such a big deal out of things. Since first meeting her and throughout our courtship, I had witnessed her receiving this message as one of twelve children. From my vantage, this night was a violation of that message in a big way. She focused on her life, relationship with her daughter, husband, son, extended family, friends, and co-workers. In fact, I experienced her yet again as more than adequate. Mellon exemplified to me and to those able to see that Julia was in the room beyond her bruised, bloated outward appearance. Julia did exist and live. Julia touched Mommy, Kevin, and me. Julia touched all of us present this night and so many others.

I know Julia continues to touch our lives today.

Chapter 23

JUST US, ONE LAST LOOK

The culmination of the evening was upon us. The transitional moment came knowing we would never see our cherished bundle of love again. Before they closed the casket for the final time it was again just the four of us alone in the room. It was our time to say thank you, I love you and goodbye to our little girl, Little Sis.

Earlier in the evening, Mellon wondered with me if this was going to be the last time she would pick Julia up and hold her. Mellon gazed down at her little girl, turned to me and tenderly shared, "I can feel the life in Julia's death like never before. Julia is so alive in me." In that moment, Mellon realized she didn't need to hold Julia one last time, as her memory of Julia's beloved life would forever be in her heart. It was okay now to close the casket and leave because we knew we were departing with Julia united forever in our living and through death. We were about to exit the funeral home for the night when Mellon let Kevin know that she was thinking of leaving Horsy the rattle and Pinky-the-Bear with Julia. Kevin immediately jumped up and ran to Julia. He retrieved both toys, declaring, "I will keep and take care of them for you."

Kevin held Horsy and Pinky dangling in his hands as he sat holding grief below the white casket before leaving Little Sis.

Chapter 24

HORSY

The following reflection was written a short while after Julia's funeral by our good friend Steve. Mellon and I had the privilege of having Steve visit with us in Boston. He was part of our inner circle of support throughout the short two weeks with Julia.

Little, Stuffed Horsy

In the grand scheme of things, I guess I don't count for much ...just a small, stuffed, yellow horsy, not much more than a handful at $5.95. But let me tell you of my friend, Julia Gene, and our short time together.

A little girl was she, precious to behold. Pink and new, soft and petite, she was so perfect a match for one so little and scruffy as me. I knew from the very beginning we were going to be the best of friends, and from her side I would not depart.

Day and night we cuddled together, amidst tubes, shunt monitors, doctors' and nurses' mini-stations. Although she never held me, I snuggled next to her face, which I kissed so gently when no one was looking. Sometimes I rested under the slightest weight of her tiny hand, hoping for the day she would squeeze me under her own power. At night, I stood guard over her like a sentinel, high above her bed where her daddy had posted me to ward off all harm.

So still she lay there, hour after hour, day after day. How glad I was to see her mommy and daddy exercise her tiny limbs, and soothe her with baby lotion whose sweet fragrance mixed with her own I wear to this day. In a matter of days, activity gave way to stillness; noise muted into silence; hope vanished into grief and loss exceeding comprehension. My infant-friend died of complications from birth.

Too soon she departed, too soon she left us, who could not imagine a future without her. One last time I nestled with my darling companion when her mommy lovingly placed me in the coffin at her side. There I felt proudest of the place I was given above all who loved her. There I felt humble and inescapably consoled by love in dozens of faces that prayerfully looked on and passed us by.

In the grand scheme of things, I guess I don't count for much...just a small, stuffed, yellow horsy, not much more than a handful at $5.95. Yet, strangely I feel a lifetime of love and worth in our short time together, me and my friend, Julia Gene.

Chapter 25

JULIA'S PLACE

DAY 4—TUESDAY

Today, our little girl was to be buried.

The graveside service was at 10:00 a.m. The sun was trying its best to peek through the heavy, darkened clouds. It had rained last night and was a damp, overcast morning with a good chance for rain. We were ready ahead of schedule. We decided to let Kevin go play on the swing set in the backyard for a while. He wore his long-sleeved pajama shirt, covered by an unbuttoned bright blue short-sleeved shirt. He wore his multicolored slacks and slip-on geometric-shaped sneakers. He put on his Mickey Mouse cap and royal blue windbreaker with a hood. He wore his now-signature protective "Wolverine" Crayola markers taped to his wrists, for if yesterday was foretelling, today would certainly be another uncertain adventure.

Mellon wore the new blue-and-white striped dress recently purchased just for this occasion. Steve wore a dark three-piece suit with tie. I wore a comfortable pair of slacks and a blue sports coat with no tie. We stood on the deck as if awaiting departure for a party or what should have been the occasion of our daughter's christening ceremony. But instead, we were going to the same cemetery we had taken Kevin often to drive through, sometimes play hide-and-go-seek, but mostly check out the cool old tombstones. But today's visit would be different.

Julia, our family, and our friends were waiting for us.

When 9:45 a.m. arrived, it was time to depart for the cemetery. Our anxiety mounted as we stepped into the big, black car. Steve and his Lincoln Town Car provided a real sense of support, safety, and security as it had during last week's earlier safe transport of Mellon to Julia's side in Boston. It was now carrying my family to Julia once again. Steve drove slowly through the streets of Agawam as we all silently prepared for the possibility of additional intimacy and connection with one another, Julia, and those who had gathered to say goodbye.

How much intimacy can I take? How much vulnerability can I endure? How much is too much? When is enough, enough? Might I find a way to sabotage the moment if I continue embracing what life offers me today? I did not talk about this as Kevin was present. I felt too vulnerable and uncertain as the car kept moving. It made its way slowly down the long driveway from the Main Street entrance of the cemetery. As we inched closer, the number of vehicles that lined the multiple cemetery roadways became almost too much to take in. So many people were here. The car was escorted to the space nearest the gravesite, which awaited our arrival. In our final few moments of privacy, we looked out the dark-tinted windows at everyone who had gathered. *Do I have to get out?* The doors finally opened, exposing our vulnerability as we become visible once again. There were so many people present from last night's wake and others present for the first time. They were all here to share their love for Mellon, Kevin, Julia, and me.

I almost couldn't take it.

Among the new faces were Mellon's older brother, Paul, and his wife, Maureen, who had traveled up from Philadelphia, stopping in Brooklyn to pick up Mellon's two younger sisters, Cathy and Jennifer. Mellon conveyed to me that she was surprised, pleased, and felt very supported by their presence, but also wondered if she deserved all this attention. My two elder uncles, Eddie and Denis (my mom's younger brothers), made the trip from Brooklyn as well. We walked past four or five rows of tombstones to get to the back row adjacent to the hedges outlining the cemetery's rear boundary.

Julia's half plot awaited us as the crowd parted in silence as we were escorted to stand above her tiny sealed white box surrounded by fresh-cut flowers.

It was a breathtaking sight.

We surrounded Julia's Place. Mellon to my right. Steve to my left. Kevin found his way into the secure and tender arms of his Uncle Mike. The supportive energy could be felt as everyone gathered closer together and began to spontaneously join hands—friends with family, family with co-workers, co-workers with neighbors, family with family—all intimately interconnecting in this treasured moment at Julia's Place. Then Kyle, our friend and minister, began the service by leading us in prayer. The moist, dark blue clouds hung just over our heads, reflecting the dark struggle we were feeling, outlined by vibrant white, puffy edges, capturing our hopefulness. The cemetery was adorned with rows of large pine trees standing tall, outlining its boundaries to the east, symbolizing the presence of all those not able to be with us at Julia's Place. More than the heavenly beauty nature offered this morning was the love I saw radiating from Mellon's eyes for her little girl. She expressed to me how the graveside service encouraged her to courageously claim the feeling that she was letting go, saying goodbye and experiencing both the end of a journey and beginning of another. This uplifted my soul to continue at a time when I was weakening and questioning my resilience.

Mellon and I both felt the deep struggle that we wouldn't be strong enough to take in the vast goodness this day offered and the opportunity to claim the genuine presence and support of all those gathered. I could see us standing together, holding one another's hands in our common grief, the ripple of love. It was a day to experience the important reality that Julia did exist, is real, and is still with us!

Midway through the service, Mellon described to me how anxious she had become, particularly with her family present, due to how visible she was leading this part of the service in reciting Julia's poem, "Bubbles."

The night before, Mellon had come and stood by my quivering side as I struggled to share the deep relationship with Julia the poem offers. Now, I was by her side, as her voice trembled with love. She later described to me her experience of reading "Bubbles": "Waves of emotion broke over me like high-tide waves relentlessly crashing on the shore. I will know Julia in a different way now. Physically, she is gone; her bubbles are no more, yet she is forever in my heart."

Not unlike "Julia's Farewell" song played the night before, this graveside service had its own movements. Culminating the crescendo of life-and-death side-by-side was singing "Salve Regina" ("Hail, Holy Queen") by three of my seminary buddies and myself. We sang this love song to the Blessed Mother in the seminary nearly every day for over a decade. Since leaving the seminary, we had not sung it together for nearly two decades. Without rehearsal, Owen plucked the first few notes out of the deepening blue sky and sang a capella the first chord: *Sal-ve, Re-gi-na*, and we joined our voices, creating a collective quiver. Our recall of the Latin hymn and words were like getting back on a bike after these many years. Arm in arm we held one another as Owen, Tom, and Steve finished off the final crescendo as my voice choked up and tears streamed down my cheeks. No rendition ever meant more to me than this one.

Mellon later captured the moment, sharing with me, "It brought me so much comfort. Your voices were so sweet, strong, and sincere. Tears flowed across the adjoining plots. Your love for the song, one another, and Julia was a fitting conclusion to the service. This was one of those precious gift moments from God. A true farewell to Julia."

An invitation to dine together at a local restaurant was made and then a final benediction sent us quietly scattering toward our vehicles. Uncle Mike tossed Kevin on his broad shoulders for a free lift back to the black car as I walked arm in arm with Mellon. I felt a strong connection and shared numbness as we walked away from our treasured gift—Julia Gene. Just at that moment, the skies opened and shed her tears on Julia's Place.

Chapter 26

THE BIG, BLACK CAR

Steve wrote another short piece about our family and the drive to the gravesite in his big, black Lincoln Town Car.

Big, Black Car

A big, black car rolls slowly and softly down the narrow cemetery drive. Tinted windows preserve the passengers' humble anonymity from all gathered, save the watchful eye of a funeral directress who ushers the vehicle to take an unexpected place of prominence. The crowd steps aside to make way for the car, forming an unrehearsed honor guard not unlike that alongside a presidential motorcade as the shiny sedan passes.

This same car—which (with great urgency only a week before) had hastened the concerned, young mother to her ailing daughter and husband's side—now serves the noble duty of funeral limousine for mother, father, brother, and friend with stayed, deliberate station. If there is such a thing as a "vocation" for a car … a certain time, a particular place, a special blend of persons and circumstances converging in one event for which only its attributes are uniquely appropriate … the big, black car fulfilled its distinguished service this mournful day.

All eyes and mounting anticipation like a spotlight are focused on the vehicle, whose stately presence boasts the dignity of its special passengers and the somber proceedings to follow. While something of a paradox telegraphs anxious messages in the crowd (who are unaccustomed to authenticity finding visible expression in even conventional terms as this formal arrival), anxiety of another sort rises inside the car from full realization of the moment at hand and the pressing crowd outside, both calling for response.

Four doors open slowly, deliberately. Passengers emerge from the privacy of quiet, personal grieving to the harsh, public exhibition of kinfolk poised to comfort. Undistracted from the real reason for their arrival, however, they proceed to the graveside, where a small, white coffin surrounded with flowers beckons them to begin their long journey of farewells to Julia Gene. And the big, black car awaits their return, to hold and carry them along the first, heartbroken miles.

Chapter 27

BEYOND JULIA'S PLACE

Traveling to the restaurant in the big, black car was both comforting and quiet. The fifteen-minute ride seemed like seconds. I wasn't sure if I was ready to enter this next part of my day. I was afraid that I would once again experience the distancing and cold reality of how my family works so hard to avoid the "pink elephant on the table." What would I be walking into? Would it be yet another frustrating experience of relationships not able to give and take? Or might the goodness from last night and this morning carry over into the restaurant? I was anxious that being myself would again be in plain sight and visible.

As it unfolded, I was indeed visible. The old (usually hurtful) family stories remained silent. Perhaps this was all due to the fact that this was a brunch and no alcohol was flowing. Maybe not. Maybe the closeness could continue being sustained among the thirty or so friends and family that had now gathered to share a meal and common purpose.

Mellon's two sisters, brother, and sister-in-law sat together with members of my immediate family around a very long table. It was at our wedding several years ago when our two families had last gathered. Despite my anxiety about the pending seating arrangements, it managed to work itself out and the conversation was authentic and kind. I thought my eyes and ears were deceiving me. Could this really be happening?

Each of my family members pulled me aside to personally express their love and sympathy for me. My two elder uncles extended the gift of paying for our meal. My grandmother thanked me for supporting her infant great-grandchildren to be part of the whole experience. She explained to me how she had never in her many years experienced the depth of both life-and-death side-by-side.

Ten or more of Mellon's co-workers shared a table and collectively embraced her at key moments throughout the meal. They shared conversation about how during Mellon's pregnancy and delivery experience they nicknamed Julia "Penelope." Get a bunch of nurses together and they could talk shop forever. Yet, on this morning, it was more than just shop-talk. They all grew closer to one another, connected through Julia's life.

The meal was over before I knew it. We were thanking our friends for being with us and for their enormous support through these very difficult days. I wondered if each of our families expected we would invite them back to our home; a house that none of them had seen or stepped into, despite numerous invitations these past three years since we moved away from Brooklyn. Mellon and I anticipated our response the night before. We decided not to invite anyone back to the house. I graciously informed everyone and once again invited a visit at another time. Surprisingly, everyone honored our decision.

Upon our return trip home in the big, black car; Kevin asked to return to the cemetery. We did, without question.

He ran out of the car ahead of us and knelt down, right inside the circle of flowers atop where Julia now lay buried. He began to cry, asking to dig up the ground so he could see his Little Sis Julia again.

Chapter 28

THE MEMORY STONE

DAY 5—WEDNESDAY: THE DAY AFTER

We traveled to our favorite outdoor restaurant with a friend, Paula, and her two children in order to do something ordinary. The day's rain had finally stopped when suddenly there appeared a magnificent rainbow spanning the vast sky. Its splendor demanded our attention and wonder. We found ourselves looking at one another.

Paula commented, "This was Julia's gift to us. She's letting us know she is safe and at peace."

I smile each time I experience the marvel of a rainbow. I stop what I'm doing and linger. I pause to reflect. Julia is at one and present within me. I hear Julia's soft voice once again whisper to me, *Slow down, Daddy, and be with me—be with me as I glow—live with me yet another day.*

A Few Days Later

Kevin's fifth birthday party was fully celebrated and went off without a hitch only a few days after Little Sis's funeral. Soon after this, a family friend offered us the use of her New York beach front summer home for a few days. This beach was where Mellon and I spent many a day. We decided to go despite Mellon coming down with a terrible chest cold. Her body had finally succumbed to the stress. The time at the beach house was very renewing. The ocean, sand, and warm sun were very comforting and restorative. I recall Mellon describing to me how she experienced the beach as "inviting happy memories of my little girl playing on the beach."

The long journey of healing was well underway for all of us and it was not uncommon to hear Mellon say she had visited Julia at the cemetery. It soon became clear that Julia's Place needed to be honored with a memorial headstone. Mellon and I had been thinking about what kind of stone we wanted and, most importantly, what we wanted to say on it. We were ready for the next steps in holding our grief and healing process.

We visited a large local chain monument store. It was as formal as the three-piece-suited salesman. He informed us that our wishes for a customized stone were not possible. He made his best sales pitch for a more formal, standard, and expensive solution. His loss. We left knowing someone out there was going to hear us and support our special request.

As we were getting in the car to leave, Mellon recalled a small place with a modest storefront in the next town over that she had passed while on a field trip with Kevin. It was calling her, or, as she later revealed, Julia was guiding her. She confidently continued, "I know where to go."

We drove straight there. Kevin grumbled a bit, thinking he was in for a long trip. We all had a totally unexpected, pleasant experience. The building appeared to be a converted home to a storefront. There were several stones on the lawn outside this exquisitely unique shop. A very pleasant young man approached us wearing dungarees and a blue work shirt. He was the owner and craftsman. He welcomed us into his shop and asked us to share our story, vision, and design. Kevin was fully engaged, showing him pictures he and I had drawn of what we thought could appear on the stone. Without a blink of an eye, the man told us, "It is no problem. I can do something like that. It would be my honor."

Kevin's smile was contagious.

It was clear the man took great pride in his custom business and loved what he did. He captured Kevin's imagination by demonstrating for us the intricate process that went into creating a personalized Memory Stone, as he called it. He was excited to hear about our desire to have a cluster of bubbles engraved alongside Kevin's sentiment written on the floral card:

You'll be with us & we'll be with you always.

We picked out a multicolored granite stone with a polished finish that would lie flat on the ground. The man invited us to come back in a few weeks to watch him create our Memory Stone.

We did just that. When Julia's stone was ready to be laid, the man informed us of the day he would be delivering it and we were there with him for that too. Meeting him was no coincidence.

Julia led us to this special man and we followed. She continues to guide paths toward life-giving relationships. She knew this was the place to create her Memory Stone of Life.

Chapter 29

JULIA'S PRESENCE

EVER AFTER

Julia's presence is felt and alive in my life.

Julia exists in my silence, listening to an inspiring song, painting a bird, writing a story, viewing a heartfelt rom-com, listening to a stranger share a sadness or joy, absorbing a beautiful sunset and rainbow, touching the hand of my beloved, smiling at the first steps of a toddler, feeling gleeful at one of my children's accomplishments, feeling pride at being the son of my living wonderful 90-year-old mother and deceased father, or feeling the joy of being a brother to five siblings with their wonderful families. I smile each time my mom responds to the question, "How many grandchildren do you have?" She proudly includes Julia each time, responding, "Seventeen with one in Heaven."

Presence invites awareness of the moment.

If you remain unaware, you may miss seizing the connections before you. Julia has taught me that being present is not a one-time deal. I remember being all wrapped up in my own stuff as she lay awaiting connection with me those first days. She knew I needed to focus on taking care of Mellon and Kevin, spending a lot of time communicating with family, and completing so many other difficult tasks just to get through those first days. One important thing Julia taught me then, and again ten years later as I first published the story of love and am still benefiting from these thirty-four years later, is that slowing down to take care of me is the secret to real living. Authentic connections follow.

In my poem "Bubbles," I wrote action words and phrases that pertain just as much to that day as they do today: *slow down, feed me, show me, nourish me, handle me with care, talk about me, Lift another time, Peek through, help me grow to live another day, freely-dream-hope to go, journey with me so slow, holding my hand, hoping to go, Come with me into Tomorrow.* I keep Julia alive in my heart through living out these words in my daily actions: some days more, some days less, but always connected.

Daddy, can you hear me?

Slow down, you are moving too fast away from what really matters right now—you! I am with you always. Stop worrying about me. My concern is that I see how you sometimes run away from your goodness. How you seem to lose the love you've gained for yourself that has enriched so many over these years. I've been watching you give so generously of yourself. Ever since I lived and died with you, you have made your life so much about giving to others. I've come to see and know that you've been that way ever since you were a little boy.

Self-sacrifice is your constant companion.

Tolerance of pain and discomfort you know all too well.

I think that's why you became a family therapist, worked in the recovery field and with those whose children died like me. You knew their suffering, and you could be with them, really be with them. Just like Mommy does too. She helps, still today, as she supports bringing life into this world. But it always doesn't work out well and she is there for all of them, like you. Knowing what it's like and uniquely able to be there with the families who need the special "Mellon" touch. You two have always been able to hold grief in your hands, supporting those in need of healing and showing them a today into tomorrow like you did with me. Even though you are not still married, you are both still one in my heart.

I marvel, Daddy, at the many different kinds of groups you led, sharing our story of love, crying every time you read "Bubbles" as if it was your first. Your courage has changed lives through keeping and sharing our story to help others live their best lives. Through Mom's and your guidance, many people who had lost a child did not give up hope and were successful having another child and growing their family. Others reconnected with family after cutting off from them because they were in so much pain and didn't understand what was happening in their relationships. Daddy, you helped them return to the light of healing.

Daddy, you have been carrying our love story for thirty-four years and now are sharing it in a book. You did what that kind lady Mary suggested in one of your columns: write a book to help people guide their journey so slow, so they can grow to live another day.

I know our Bubble actions can be theirs too.

Daddy, it's your time to grow, to slow down and grow to live another day. Thank Mommy and Kevin for all their love and support. My love to Hannah, Aidan, and Connor—the best sibs a big Sis could ever have!

Bubbles

Blow me a bubble or two…
Lift your chest, another time
Peek through your windows to life
and show me your true baby blue colors.

Drain and drip fluid child
Pee just another CC for us.
P waves speak to me of rhythm,
149, 159, 169, – slow down –
the EKG of life shifting…
not too high, not too low.

Little bubbles, pop for Daddy.
Show me your strength of eight long days.
You've been poked and probed,
suctioned and stitched,
opened and finally closed.

Tubes of life handled with care,
nourish me, feed me, as I await
Mommy's vanilla shakes.

Talk about me and help me grow,
grow to live another day,
when my bubbles
can freely blow.

Today
is my
challenge

to pump
and blow;

Tomorrow
is my dream date…
I hope to go.

Come with me
on my journey so slow;
come, hold my hand as I blow.

Tuesday 5/28/91—Daddy

I want to thank Mellon and Kevin for holding grief with me. My heart is filled with gratitude for their contributions in living, giving, and sharing Julia's story of love.

We are truly blessed to have Julia in our lives. We are grateful to share our precious little one with you. People often ask how many children I have. Mellon and I proudly include Julia as one of our five children. Julia's siblings include her as well when asked the same question. We claim this opportunity to share Julia's special presence in our lives. While some people express discomfort with the news of an infant death, most engage in affirming her presence and even share their own story with us. What a gift to connect with people in this way.

We welcome Julia's continued presence as we hold grief and share the blessings of our ripples of love.

Julia Gene
5.21.91–6.1.91

Messages from Julia's Siblings

From youngest brother Connor Joseph:
"Love Ya."

From younger brother Aidan Daniel:

Dear Julia,
Being the middle brother was a great way to grow up. I'm very lucky in that regard. Now I'm not saying that having older siblings wasn't great... it certainly was. I just can't help but think how much better growing up with an additional older sister would have been, not only for myself but for my other siblings. Plus, it would have been fun to have a bit more competition in the favorite child category.

I often contemplate what it would have been like seeing you and Hannah have the type of relationship I share with my brothers. Not that her and I don't get along, there's just something about that sister-sister bond I know she would have cherished.

I also frequently wonder what your relationship with our parents would have looked like, where you'd be living these days, what career you would've had a calling for, what music you would've gravitated towards and all the random things you would've influenced me to enjoy. One of the many perks of having older siblings is the access to free knowledge, that is of course, if you're willing to pay close enough attention. I can honestly say that was one thing I never passed up.

It saddens me to think about all the advice and lessons I would've learned from you. I'm sure there would have been a few gems. Now just because I didn't grow up with you doesn't mean you didn't teach me anything, I just had to look a little deeper. In fact, I feel as though you played a major role in teaching me one of the most important things in life; the ability to love. To this day, I don't think I fully harness what the effect of losing you had on our parents, but I know one thing for certain, they loved you and always will. They were selfless parents and poured all their love for you into raising us. I will never forget the countless trips with Mom to freshen up your flowers and the joy on her face every time she catches a glimpse of her favorite bird that reminds us of you. Your time here created a beautiful ripple effect for which I am forever grateful.

Love,
Aidan

From younger sister Hannah Lory:

As the only living female child of my parents surrounded by three brothers, I have often stopped to wonder how different my life would have been like had Julia continued living. What would it have been like to grow up with an older sister? Would I have had someone to steal clothes from? Would we have gotten along or would that two-year age gap be just annoying enough for us to butt heads all the time? Would she have taught me how to put on makeup? Would we have gossiped about boys? Would we have shared any friends? I'll never really know the answers to those questions, but that is okay. I've now had the additions of sisters-in-law to my life and they have given me a small taste of what it could have been like having an older sister.

Throughout my childhood, my parents always talked to us about Julia and we would bring cupcakes to the cemetery each year to celebrate her birthday. I used to regularly visit with my mother as she would garden around her gravestone or we would all just visit after a Sunday church service. I've never truly felt the loss of Julia the same way my parents and older brother have, as I was not alive while she was. Her spirit has always seemed like she was with us as my parents kept her alive through their voices and their actions. To this day, Julia still has a handmade stocking hung by the chimney for Christmas each year. She must be on the good list in heaven because Santa still always leaves her something in that stocking!

As I near my 32nd birthday, it is strange to think about how I am around the same age as my parents when they experienced this loss. Whenever I near a birthday, I always find myself having a thought about what age Julia would have been turning in a few short months after my birthday. What would she have been like? In a way, I am happy that our birthday months are so close together. I'm happy that I was able to give my parents a fairly regular pregnancy and birthing experience after the trauma Julia's short life had brought about. I think I'll always be grateful that they were able to move forward from that and continue on to have me and my two younger brothers.

Having grown up in a household where my family was open about talking about Julia unknowingly taught me at a young age that you aren't guaranteed a long life and should make the most of the one that you are living. I think it's great they have been so open with their friends, the world and shared their experience as it can only help others who have gone through something similar. It's nice not to feel like you are alone in something. I hope that this book will be able to do just that and that Julia would be happy to know her story will live on even though she was taken from us too soon.

From older brother Kevin Edward:

Most of what I remember about my sister and the experience of her passing stems from photos and family tales. As the only child at the time, I was very excited to be a big brother since I come from a family of six on one side and twelve on the other. Being so young at the time of Julia's birth, complications and death, most of the gravity of the situation was well over my head. It forced me to deal with death at a very early age (having never had a pet or other family member pass during my lifetime that I was connected to). I remember the trips to the hospital in Boston, staying with our neighbors Nancy and Debbie. It was exciting to "sleep over" somewhere I'd never been, although it was just across the street, but not knowing why or for how long was a lingering question for my little brain.

While I don't remember holding Julia in the hospital after birth, the family photo has always held powerful weight for my parents. Whenever I see it, I'm hit with a wave of "What If" scenarios and how has that early experience with death laid its imprint on me without my conscious knowledge. Seeing characters, beloved or new, in film or stories always seems to hit a nerve of sadness and I always seem to cry before anyone else in the room. Sometimes I wonder if it stems from Julia; from caring about someone with only limited physical exposure, but losing it so quickly and unexpectedly. Maybe it was seeing something so innocent and precious slip away so quickly that surfaces, or maybe I'm just a sappy audience.

The funeral service was a difficult day, seeing all my loved ones and family truly sad for the first time. I remember feeling deep sadness like nothing ever before or since. My parents give me a ton of credit for the connection and experience with the gravestone and engraving. I remember feeling valued and vindicated in my feelings at the time. Whenever it's brought up it's still nice to know I contributed something special to a time when my parents were grieving even though I couldn't heal their pain. My birthday was a few days after Julia's passing and I only remember it because my parents have brought it up. Most of my young birthdays at the house bleed together, however I have no specific recollection of that specific one besides seeing my parents happy.

The next time my mom was pregnant I recall being concerned and more interested in learning what happened last time. Today I always say I am the oldest of five siblings, which almost always is followed by a minor recap that Julia counts, especially when I'm talking to students. I've found it's a nice way to open the door to my personal life, show some vulnerability and my willingness to share hard truth so they can do the same. Some students have shared their experience with losing a loved one or sibling in the aftermath of that story. My fifth-grade teacher Mr. Spiro pulled me aside one day to tell me how much he enjoyed reading my father's columns in the newspaper.

A message from Julia's grandmother:

Kevin, Hannah, and Aidan knew the experience of my mother's gentle touch and love. Her name to them was Nannie. My name for her was Julia, Mom. I was so pleased to hear Daniel and Mary Ellen named their second child Julia after my mother and Gene after my husband, Eugene. However, it got confusing for Kevin, calling my mother Nannie along with all his cousins and also calling me Nannie, especially while my mom was still with us up until 1999. So, together Kevin and I created my new name—Sheilagram. After all, he was hearing everyone around him calling me Sheila, so it became something natural for him to copy. Thus, I became Sheilagram and his great-grandmother remained Nannie—Julia.

I loved the idea of Kevin, Hannah, Aidan, and Connor knowing their sister was named Julia after my mother. Julia was an independent, loving, caring, strong, and resilient woman who went through many challenges; least of which was immigrating as a little girl from Scotland and raising nine children of her own. She often had to work out of the home to help make ends meet. I am the oldest of nine, now the matriarch of the family after accepting the baton, as it were, from my mother. Naming and passing on our roles is an important point Dan talks about in this book. I am so happy to have experienced firsthand Dan's loving courage within this larger story of love and his *Let's Talk About It* newspaper columns within it. He could have left out all the parts of his story that were challenging to face, but then we would have missed out on a more fulsome telling of our family legacy which makes us who we are today. After all, we are all shaped by the power of family—for good and not so good—as Dan so vividly depicts.

I have encouraged Dan's living in the moment and writing this book. I am so fortunate to have read it. I have loved him as tenderly and affectionately as I am able, as I faced similar challenges as did my mother. I too had to work out of the home to help make ends meet and I was also challenged by marrying a good man who struggled with alcohol use. The effects of which impacted me, my siblings, and my six children. Some of those experiences are difficult to face, some captured in these pages, especially when the centuries-old "Irish" message echoes within: "do *not* talk about it" and "it never happened." Dan has my full support to talk about his story as part of our larger family story. I trust him as he faithfully recalls how it impacted him and I'm sure influenced us all. I experience sadness hearing him describe the many challenges in his story and columns, but I am so proud and happy he is doing the hard work of "breaking the generational cycle" that has limited far too many of us.

Dan's tender touch is what I've always known. He knows love and fortunately or unfortunately, as it were, the role of being "in the middle." He has always been so sensitive to others. My joy in reading this book is seeing him learn to use his sensitivity and ability to love "himself" and how that love and connection is shared with so many others. I see his healing process and am privileged he has shared his trauma stories with me. It was hard for me at times to listen to his experiences knowing, as a mother, how I wished I were there to stop—and protect—my little boy from such pain and discomfort. I am so glad he trusted me with his stories despite his worry about how I would take knowing his truth. He and I have spent our lifetime talking about our truths. We often share our tears together as we both grow and heal. As his book so beautifully depicts: it's about learning to intimately love your "self" and share that love with others.

Julia Gene knew Dan's story. She lived out her own challenges with him, her mother, and big brother. Dan's whole family truly live their story of love. I for one am so proud to be part of a legacy of intimate moments in life-and-death side-by-side.

—Sheilagram

A poem from Daddy:
September 7, 2025

Tangled Up

Losing a child, life becomes tangled up,
all turned 'round, inside-out and upside-down.
I know the give and take that turns it inside-out, upside-down,
and all-around.

Snap the light back on.
Usher in the heart of self,
bestow what I most need,
back together with Thee.

I am not alone.
Walk with me,
let the light glow and flow
to grow still another day.

Even if the deserted light flickers unaided,
follow it.
See your way forward moving backwards
turned inside-out, upside-down, and all 'round.

Look back and forth again and again
turned all 'round, inside-out and upside-down.
Gaze in each moment shifting right to left,
up to down, inside-out and all turned around.

Battered and bruised we seek relief
all turned 'round, inside-out, and upside-down
believing today affords healing
as we persist in holding grief.

Essence is being in the moment called today
all turned 'round, inside-out, and upside-down
keen on holding restorative grief,
reconciling within tears of enmity.

I can't float alone turned all 'round.
Together we hold hands for free
knowing what's down is up, in is out and
living requires being all turned around.

Your holding hands bestow vitality
in my inside-out, upside-down all turned around.
Goodness is claimed stabilizing space and time
inside-out, upside-down and all turned 'round.

Lead and guide me
to share new lands,
tangled upside-down, inside-out
and all turned 'round.

I have discovered
you are the Way.
You provide fulfilling life
inside-out, upside-down and all turned around.

Illuminate the way.
Shine your Truth
guiding me
in the darkest of days.

Gratitude
is my constant companion;
without her,
I would be lost.

Compassion defines my way
embracing being turned all 'round
found in the shadows
within inside-out and upside-down.

Tolerance for "what is"
taunts my soul.
Freedom lies within change
nourishing a clear distorted way.

Chains are meant to be broken,
unenslaved by living and death.
Life comes of age when I burrow in
upside-down, inside-out and all turned 'round.

Twist and turns know no bounds;
sustaining
a life
inside-out, upside-down and turned all-around.

Draw near and consider
our new life provision,
unmistakably distinct from a perch
upside-down, inside-out and all turned 'round.

Life is for free
and death the price.
Death of Thee
for life with me.

Walking with Thee
is a duty-bound
in love
found.

A strength
comes our way
embracing being all turned 'round
inside-out and upside-down.

Give resistance away
as you make your way.
Disperse your brilliant light
along the twisted path without dim.

Sparkle and give away
abundance
as it emanates
from the lost and found.

You and I are forged in grace to live a life
all turned around, inside-out and upside-down.
The path is new,
so are you.

Claim then
for your own
being turned all 'round,
lost then found inside-out and upside-down.

You are not alone in this recovery
upside-down, inside-out and all turned 'round;
for here is where you can truly turn your life
outside-in and flipped around.

Thank you for showing a way
to hold despair and pain;
holding grief in our hands is
the Way, the Truth and the Life.

For whomever
comes to Me
can live all turned 'round
inside-out and upside-down.

I am now walking the Way.
Julia Gene, I love you
for turning my life inside-out,
upside-down and all-around.

—Daddy

Written and inspired by a 4 a.m. dream waking only to remember being with Julia and the feeling of being tangled up.

Let's walk together with vitality…

PART TWO

Book Club Discussion—A Reflective Listening Leadership Book Club Model

BOOK CLUB OVERVIEW

As you'll recall from the Introduction, this process follows the listening model established by Carl Rogers. The goal in the context of conducting a book club group is twofold:

1. For the Speaker the goal is to be heard and have the experience of being listened to. The Speaker should come away with a real sense that what has been stated is important and valued by the Listeners.

2. For the Listeners, on the other hand, the goal is to experience how hard and worthwhile it is to actively listen. This requires both separating out and caring for what gets raised in themselves, while still being able to track and provide feedback to what the Speaker is saying. Listeners learn, if they didn't already know, the value and importance of making the other person most important, hearing them, and providing their best feedback.

Demonstrating real presence in the moment is invaluable and something that will provide a true give-and-take experience for all.

How It Works

(Speaker)—When the prompt topic or question is claimed by the

Speaker, they have the floor to make their observation, briefly tell their story, and most importantly, comment on the topic or question at hand about the book that is before the group. The Speaker's statement should reflect their life, feelings, and/or experiences regarding the material under review. The Speaker's comments are generally held to no longer than 5–10 minutes, but this can be negotiated and/or predetermined by the group beforehand and overseen by the facilitator.

(Listener(s))—The Listener does not interrupt the Speaker while they present their comments. Listeners listen to the Speaker without outward reaction within the group. The Listener's main goal is to do the difficult task of real listening and not react or communicate their personal experience or what they share in common, etc.

We accomplish this through several different tools or techniques to provide "Reflective Feedback." The Listener should focus on what the Speaker says via their emotional and/or nonverbal cues, pausing for the moment their own immediate reaction(s) and knowing that later there will be a time and space to address these, either outside the group or when it is their turn as Speaker. But for now, they are a Listener.

Generally, Listener feedback is brief—around 2 to 5 minutes. It is thoughtful, precise, and does not attempt to restate everything the Speaker said. Instead, it addresses in general a few specifics that the Listener believes capture important points of the presentation. The feedback avoids being duplicative of another Listener's feedback already given. The Listener should simply acknowledge that the same or similar point of feedback has already been shared by someone, without repeating the full point, and continue on with their unique points. It is always helpful for the Listener to authentically state what they believe the Speaker did well in their presentation.

Key Characteristics & Principles of Reflective Listening

Additional information is available via an internet search to gain greater understanding of Rogers' Reflective Listening specific tools and techniques and other beneficial contemporary outgrowths of his model.

The following characteristics and principles of reflective listening are guides or tools to help you focus on how best to provide your feedback. Review each one, understand yourself in the process, and ultimately determine, based on the complexity of the Speaker's presentation material, how best to use one or more of the tools to demonstrate that the Speaker has been heard.

A helpful tip: Write down key points and/or observations the Speaker states or emotions they demonstrate. This can help provide the most accurate feedback. Listening is difficult and active note-taking honors the process.

- Express understanding of the Speaker's message in their own words.
- Show respect and acceptance for the Speaker by remaining neutral and non-judgmental.
- Be open-minded even if disagreeing with the Speaker by thinking reflectively and being open to what the Speaker has to say.
- Use reflective statements more often than questions, ideally at least twice as many.
- Use a variety of reflections, like a simple reflection that repeats or rephrases what the Speaker says, as well as complex reflections, like using different words to reflect the underlying meaning.

- Avoid paraphrasing by summarizing what the Speaker said using their own words.
- Allow the Speaker to finish their thoughts or opinions without interrupting.
- Ask questions of the Speaker to elaborate where necessary.
- Avoid interrogation by not asking question after question without offering your reflections.
- Reflect back to the Speaker the feelings you observed.
- Be specific by choosing specific information to reflect on.
- Let the Speaker lead by supporting them to decide what's best for them.
- Check in with the Speaker after providing your feedback to see if what you said resonates or not. Let them decide if it fits or needs further modification.

Feedback to the Feedback

Upon hearing each Listener provide their feedback, it is now the Speaker's responsibility to respond by either:

1. affirming what the Listener stated was accurate;

2. qualifying the Listener's statement by responding how it slightly missed the mark, then filling in the missing piece/gaps; or

3. stating there has been a misunderstanding in the Listener's feedback and simply reclarifying their original statement around the apparent specific misunderstood point. *(This is not a time for debate or argument between folks—just clarification of the Speaker's position and/or intent).

Feedback-to-the-feedback time should be a positive experience for the Listener to hear the Speaker's feedback to their feedback. The Speaker should politely thank the Listener in some manner indicating closure to that exchange and their readiness to move to the next Listener's feedback. A different Reflective Feedback option will hopefully be utilized by the next Listener to provide variety to the Speaker and the group.

The Role of the Facilitator

Not all Listeners need provide feedback to each Speaker. This can be predetermined ahead of time or determined in real-time management. Equal sharing of contribution by participants is important to monitor, so that no one person outweighs the group participation. I would recommend doing one Listener's feedback and then the Speaker's feedback-to-the-feedback, then moving to the next Listener's feedback and repeating the process as you determine. Establish a group facilitator for each gathering (taking turns would be helpful) to have someone:

1. monitor the dynamics of the group size,
2. adhere to the group focus as determined at the end of the previous group,
3. guide what the next group focus will entail so that folks come prepared for the next meeting,
4. guide the movement of the Reflective Feedback among all participants (if needed),

5. track and guide (if needed) the Reflective Feedback to assure it is nonjudgmental and not interpretative (expressing one's personal opinion on how someone else "should" act),

6. manage the predetermined structured or unstructured time set aside by members, and

7. negotiate flexibility of the above with group members as desired, and

8. manage any other matters that arise.

Book Club Questions & Guidance

Book Club #1: You in Recovery?
Let's start here:

1. The author's answer to the question "You in recovery?" "Aren't we all in recovery for something?" What does this provoke in you?

2. Can you or do you side with the female patient who challenges the author to be seen? How is she able to see him, invite him, and be so present with him in that moment not knowing where he is going? How do you relate to her? What does she "touch off" in you?

3. Can one be "in recovery" due to grieving the death of a loved one? If so, in what ways? If limited, how so? If not, how come?

4. Other discussion points

Book Club #2: Nothing to Say
Let's start here:

1. Have you ever felt or thought you have nothing to say; as if you had no voice and even if you had a voice, you shouldn't speak up and use it? Or somehow it was okay for others (to try) to silence you?

2. Do you experience a buried inside thought that questions and maybe even believes that you are a fraud? And at times, simultaneously, knowing that this current version of who you are and have worked so hard to become is real and not a fraud? Is thinking you are a fraud the real fraud or is becoming who you are what is most real in your life?

3. In hindsight, what was your experience of reading this column seeing how the author used it up front to open the book? Is there a connection to be made between on one hand the (family system) message that the author has nothing to say while on the other hand capably filling a book with "I DO have something to say" as evidenced by his story of love and change? Can you speak to the juxtaposition of "nothing" and "abundance" in your life?

4. Other discussion points

Book Club #3: I Do
Let's start here:

1. What is your experience of the author's "just cause" action?

2. Have you ever felt alone giving voice to something you were keeping down/not remembering/not wanting to see the light of day?

3. The theme of "visibility" is important. Have you experienced being invisible to yourself or another? What does visibility look like?

4. Discuss the prompts "moved the problem," "out of sight, out of mind," and "it never happened."

5. What are your "I DO" self-affirmations?

6. Other discussion points

Book Club #4: The Scent of Self
Let's start here:

1. Can you smell yourself?

2. Do you know the difference between the "scent-of-self" and the "familial scent"?

3. Is being an individual possible? Is change possible? Is it possible to be free to live *both* connected to *and* separate from your family?

4. Other discussion points

Book Club #5: The Problem with Goodness
Let's start here:

1. What is the problem with goodness in your life?

2. Are you able to own both your achievements and mistakes? If so, how do you do this?

3. Do you agree with the author's three elements of this problem? Are there others?

4. Other discussion points

Book Club #6: Poem Reviews

- Discuss poems "Bubbles" and "Tangled Up"

Book Club #7: Chapter Discussion

- Discuss *Holding Grief: A Dad's Memoir*

Each chapter offers a unique opportunity to focus on the details of the story line, character development, struggles and accomplishments, setbacks and achievements, exhilaration and disappointments, life-and-death side-by-side. I invite you to take each chapter and review it alone, then open up to one another about the above components and more. Let it speak to you. Review your personal notes captured in real time and share what touches your soul, your mind, your story. Talk about what is written and what you long to say. Speak to the courage to face the unknown; the uncertainty of what life certainly offers and, in some ways, forces you to face, alone and together.

Each chapter taps into different emotional aspects of what it means to be alive and hold grief in your hands. Allow what resonates in you and share this with the group. The story unfolds moving through different timeframes (past, present, and future—the *El*

Olam) describing and demonstrating the roles learned and played out in our growing-up family of origin and our family of choice. Be mindful of your own roles as they become evident and work to change them. As you read the author's story of love and newspaper columns, be aware of your own stories that emerge within you, those that don't want to re-emerge, and then consider talking about it.

Each chapter offers an opportunity to claim a separate book club gathering, but the group may of course elect to cluster a few chapters together or review the book in total. Discuss among yourselves how you'd like to proceed and be flexible as you go, knowing that this is your time and your group to make your own. So, enjoy the journey together, supporting individual learning and growth along the way.

SOURCES

Haas, David. "Come and Journey with Me." On *Come and Journey* by David Haas, Marty Haugen, and Michael Joncas. GIA Publications, 1995.

Kulik, Buzz, dir. *Brian's Song*. Columbia Pictures, 1971.

Mumford & Sons. "The Cave." On *Sigh No More*. Island Records, 2009.

Rogers, Carl R. *On Becoming a Person: A Therapist's View of Psychotherapy*. Houghton Mifflin Company, 1961.

Shaiman, Marc, comp. "Julia's Farewell." In *Heart and Souls*, dir. Ron Underwood. Universal Pictures, 1993.

Spielberg, Steven, dir. *Saving Private Ryan*. DreamWorks and Paramount Pictures, 1998.

ABOUT THE AUTHOR

Dan Pender, MA, MFT

Dan Pender exceled on the baseball diamond and hardcourt despite his small frame, but struggled within the classroom, his circle of friends and family. He 'ran away' to the catholic seminary high school fleeing the middle role and function within his family of eight. After leaving the religious life he managed to replicate his middle role by becoming an account executive in the advertising field, in his Wall Street brokerage role, becoming a family therapist and advocate for those sexually abused by catholic priests. The ladder part of his career he was a substance use disorder and behavioral health staff member, program director, clinical supervisor that culminated as a Vice President of his regional agency before retiring. He co-raised five children and successfully supported four of them through college. One child, Julia Gene, lived a short and abundant life. *Holding Grief* is a story of love that includes older brother and mom's intimate relationship through life-and-death side-by-side with little 'sis' and his daughter.

www.ingramcontent.com/pod-product-compliance
Lightning Source LLC
Chambersburg PA
CBHW030924060726
47591CB00005B/1659

9781966981244